AUTUMN LEAVES *&* GOLDEN DAYS

Autumn Leaves &
Golden Days

DAVID EDELSTEN

Illustrated by
BECKY UNWIN

THE DOVECOTE PRESS

First published in 2011 by The Dovecote Press Ltd
Stanbridge, Wimborne Minster, Dorset BH21 4JD

ISBN 978-1-904-34995-2

Text © David Edelsten 2011
Illustrations © Becky Unwin 2011

David Edelsten and Becky Unwin have asserted their rights under the Copyright,
Designs and Patent Act 1988 to be identified as authors of this work

Designed by The Dovecote Press
Printed and bound in Spain by GraphyCems, Navarra

All papers used by The Dovecote Press are natural,
recyclable products made from wood grown in sustainable,
well-managed forests

A CIP catalogue record for this book is available
from the British Library

1 3 5 7 9 8 6 4 2

Contents

Foreword

Mrs Anthony Pitt-Rivers
LORD-LIEUTENANT OF DORSET

David Edelsten is a true son of Dorset who, for many years, has written of his love of his family and the countryside where lives and his occasional, rather reluctant, trips to London. In these delightful and thoughtful pieces, first published as a diary in the magazine *Dorset Life*, he takes us round his village and along the byways of Dorset, often seen from the back of a favourite horse and accompanied by a much-loved dog.

He tells us of local events and dramas past and present, meets friends and neighbours, many of whom he has known all his life, and reminds us of places to revisit or discover for ourselves.

Brigadier Edelsten reminisces about many aspects of his life and his military career and we learn that he has always had a healthy disregard for the 'bureaucrats' and those who impose their uninformed ideas on places he knows and loves.

Autumn Leaves & Golden Days, with its charming illustrations by Becky Unwin, invites you to share a reflective journey through the seasons and I am sure that this is a journey which all who love country life, and especially those who share his passion for Dorset, will follow with the greatest pleasure.

Valerie Pitt-Rivers

Spring

Running for the Train

Since I'm never late and have never before in my life overslept, how come I didn't wake up on the morning of the State Opening of Parliament until 25 minutes before my train was due to leave Sherborne station – Sherborne being, in normal times, all of a twenty-minute drive away? Was some gremlin at work in my subconscious, determined that I should not take the place so improbably reserved for me in the Royal Gallery of the House of Lords?

I shan't soon forget that drive. The worst bit was the feeling that the level crossing barriers would certainly descend on, or just in front of, my car bonnet as I raced down the oddly-named Gas House Hill towards them. In fact they dropped just behind me, and for a down train. I had five minutes to park the car, run a razor over my face and grab a beaker of coffee from what is surely the best station café in the whole world before leaping onto my train, tie and cuffs-links flying, for a very disordered and hungry journey.

* * *

Whitehall that morning was overrun with smiling and helpful police who, once they had scanned the important pasteboard in my hand and were satisfied that I was who I said I was, patiently helped me zigzag through a chicane of barriers across Parliament Square to my destination: Old Parliament Yard, through the Norman Porch, into the House of Lords and up the Sovereign's Staircase.

If you are wondering why this country mouse was being

treated like Lord Muck, it is because I'm lucky enough to be writing the history of the Queen's Bodyguard, the Honourable Corps of Gentlemen at Arms, founded by Henry VIII 500 years ago this year. They kindly arrange for me to watch them at work occasionally. It is part of what other kind friends call my 'research', in other words the all-too-brief period of frantic panic that usually comes between the arrival of a journalistic commission and its deadline. In fact I have plenty of time for this book and am enjoying writing it immensely.

The Royal Gallery is like an enormous gilded, painted and bejewelled casket, turned outside-in. My seat was at the foot of a massive bronze statue of Henry V and all around were full-length portraits: my *vis-à-vis* was that shy hero of my boyhood, King George VI, in Garter robes. My immediate neighbour was Mistress Wales, as the charming wife of Wales Herald Extraordinary is known. With introductions and kindly explanations she made my morning as easeful as finding myself in such a place at such a time could possibly be.

How can I convey to you the magic and glamour of the next hour? A tramp, tramp, tramp off-stage, a sound that would have had me cowering under my seat at a horror film, announced that a dismounted detachment of the Household Cavalry in their heavy knee-boots was taking post on the Sovereign's Staircase. Having completed their search of the cellars in case a latter-day Guy Fawkes should have been at work, the Yeomen of the Guard entered the Gallery and lined its aisle, followed a few minutes later by the Gentlemen at Arms, complete with their ancient pole-axes.

At 10.52 – every item in the programme was precisely timed – the Crown Imperial was placed on a table not a horse's length from where I sat, and at 11.01 was borne by the Lord Great Chamberlain into the Robing Room. Meanwhile the Heralds had assembled, splendid in their tabards. Then the Queen arrived, passing almost within touching distance as we made our bows and bobs.

I think that my most lasting impression is of the style of it all, the grace under pressure, the lack of fuss: that and the unstuffiness of all concerned. The Earl Marshal, the Duke of Norfolk, with a word and a smile for everybody, had of course the full weight of the occasion on his shoulders, but you never would have guessed it; I saw him glance at his wrist-watch no more than perhaps twice, ditto the Lord Great Chamberlain, a mere boy to my old man's eyes.

* * *

The journey home was everything that the journey up was not. At Salisbury, where the train divided, two pretty ladies boarded for Exeter, seating themselves beside and across from me. I don't know how it is that one always gets into conversation with pretty ladies, or how they wormed out of me all the details of the proud excitements of my day, but so it happened and I could not have enjoyed the journey more. My last memory is of them giggling at my bowler hat as I bade them 'Good night'.

MARCH 2009

Echo of the Raj

If you've done it yourself, or seen it done a dozen times, please don't write in, but I claim to be the only person in the history of the human race who has carried a barometer any distance on horseback. Not just one of those little barometers, like a monocle staring at you off the lobby wall, but banjo-shaped and half the size of a warming pan.

It happened like this. Ollie and I were up on the ridgeway, on that track above Buckland Newton where Tess walked . . . where, for me, she still walks. There was this unlikely thing lying discarded on the grass verge. Its weight came as a surprise. Made of some very dark, close-grained wood – teak, I suppose – it was heavy beyond its bulk. The face was missing, but its surface was decorated with a chaste white floral pattern. I tied it to the saddle-Ds with the binder-twine I always carry and struggled back on board.

It hung there as if it were a cavalry trooper's sabre, bumping against Ollie's ribs. A lot of horses I have known would have objected strongly, but not Ollie. He hallucinates about storm drains, imagines all sorts of non-existent roadside horrors, but is apparently completely phlegmatic about barometers, just as he's bomb-proof in traffic.

What was its history? I wondered as we walked home. My guess is that it was made in India, long ago, haggled over in a street bazaar. Was it brought home proudly by some soldier or other servant of the Empire, worshipped as a household god by generations of children, consulted anxiously when the weather mattered, then somehow broken, and dumped in that precious spot, a small symptom of what I have come to think of as 'the death of shame'? How can people bring themselves to do such things?

* * *

A few days later, Ollie's fantasies about drains suddenly came true. I'll tell you the story exactly as it happened, without ornament: see if you can believe, let alone understand it.

We were walking soberly down Park Lane, the narrow road that curls over the shoulder of Dungeon Hill in the final descent from the Dorset Downs to the Blackmore Vale and home. Ollie suddenly went into thunderstruck mode, and with reason. Where there should have been a drain there was a hole big enough to lose a dog or baby down, with a chasm beneath it. 'I told you so,' Ollie might have said. Coaxing him by, I hastened home and e-mailed the Council, describing the hole and exactly where it was: so much for Tuesday, Day 1.

That evening came the following e-mail ding-dong. Them: 'We will unfortunately need more precise location information

for the fault. Were there any landmarks nearby, eg. pubs etc?'
Me (getting shirty): 'I have named the road, given its number
and the grid square. I am shocked that you have had no-one out
there immediately.'

Day 2, Wednesday, brings a blizzard of mails from three
different directions, some of them four pages long, one
addressing me fondly by my first name. Amongst them was this
beauty: 'Thank you . . . for supplying us with much more specific
information [I didn't!]. I have reported this to our highways
team and they will attend within the next hour.'

I relaxed, duty done – silly me. On Day 3, Thursday, giving
myself a treat, I rode Bella. She's scatty but adorable, a typical
chestnut mare. Home-bred, she's more or less retired, but just
occasionally for old times' sake I throw a saddle over her. We
rode north out of the village, scampered over Dungeon and
walked home by Park Lane. The hole was just as Ollie and I had
found it, unmarked, dangerous.

Losing my rag, I asked at the end of a short rant, 'What is
going on?' That evening came the news that the surveyors had
walked the road and could find no hole. I went out and, hoping
that 'they' would not confiscate it, put one of my precious,
somehow acquired traffic cones on the hole, confident that at
last something would be done.

Come Friday, Day 4, the weekend upon us: no change,
nothing, and by the next morning my cone had been stolen. To
cut a very long story short, it took umpteen e-mails and sixteen
days before that dangerous drain was made safe.

As chance would have it, on Day 4, when I was in a high
rage, the lunchtime wireless news carried a report that a Lord
Jones had told a Select Committee of the House of Commons,
'The job of government could be done by half the numbers.' It
is a timely thought as we glumly scan our new Council Tax bills
and wonder how we will ever manage to pay them during the
'Brownturn'.

APRIL 2009

Dancing with Jane Austen

'Don't horses sometimes make monkeys of us?' Diana exclaimed over lunch, when we were talking through my morning's misadventure on Dungeon Hill. Ollie, taking a fancy to an inviting patch of mud, and for once betraying my loose-rein trust in him, had suddenly got down to roll. It's a pony trick, but I've never known a horse do it. It was as much as I could manage to quit the stirrups and jump clear. We were on the fairly steep side of the hill and the thought of being caught underneath him was quite alarming.

Seeing me on my feet, he got to his and scarpered, full gallop, stopping only when he got to the wicket gate into Great Wootton Wood, the nearest route home. 'Shells' is an enormous meadow, all but forty acres, draped like a cape over Dungeon's western shoulder. I'm very fond of it in the normal way, but trudging through the full length of its deep mud, the best part of half a mile to the road, with Ollie showing no sign of coming to hand, I'd soon had enough of it.

In my experience, loose horses on their own, when they have got over being 'silly bold', as my mother used to call naughty children, value security more than freedom and soon come to hand – but not Ollie on this occasion. After waiting in the lane for half an hour or so, I plodded crossly home, picking up litter as I went, until a kindly North Dorset District Council lorry driver offered me a lift.

I saddled Ollie's stable-mate, the irresistible Bella, rode back and collected him. Sure enough, he came trotting towards us, whinnying pathetically, as soon as we came into his anxious view. He hadn't rolled – thank goodness, as that would have been very expensive in the saddlery department – and his reins, by some lucky fluke, had double-looped themselves round his neck out of harm's way.

Ollie's wild hillside fandango in the deep mud left him lame on his dodgy leg next day and off-games for half a week, but otherwise no harm was done.

* * *

Diana's contra-evolutionary lunchtime remark, seeming to suggest a return to our simian origins, put me in mind of the great Charles Darwin, the bicentenary of whose birth we celebrate this year. In all the media coverage I have yet to hear mention of, let alone credit given to, the Dorset man who first set Darwin's foot on the path to formulating his theory of the Origin of Species. I refer to the great Victorian naturalist and publisher, John Gould, who, in a well-recorded 'eureka' moment for Darwin, suggested the significance of the variations in the finches he had brought back from the Galapagos Islands in HMS *Beagle*.

Gould was born at Lyme Regis on 14 September 1804. By chance we have a description of his birthday because the only surviving letter that Jane Austen wrote from Lyme bears that date. She swam that morning, she told her sister Cassandra, 'stayed in rather too long . . . shall be more careful another time.' On the previous evening she had been to a ball, when 'an odd-looking man who had been eyeing me for some time . . . at last, without any introduction, asked me if I meant to dance again.'

Sometime in that busy 24 hours, somewhere nearby, a humble gardener's wife, Mrs Gould, gave birth to a son. Born into poverty, almost, and humbly schooled, he was to become one of the great men of science of his day. He was to produce some of the finest ornithological books ever seen. Gould lives still in his wonderful bird pictures and his tombstone bears the simple legend, 'The Bird Man'. Goodness

knows where it is now, but I remember as a boy being shown, still in its presentation box, a gold-mounted seal given to him as a token of appreciation by a fellow naturalist, Prince Charles Lucien Bonaparte, nephew of Napoleon I.

However fulfilled, John Gould's can scarcely have been a happy life. His wife, Elizabeth, a fine illustrator in her own right, died shortly after the birth of their sixth child to survive infancy, and two of his three sons pre-deceased him.

His only grandchild, my father's mother, died in this house, bringing the Gould story full circle back to Dorset. If no-one else remembers John Gould's contribution to Charles Darwin's world-altering achievement, it is not forgotten in his birthplace.

MAY 2009

Signs of the Times

What bureaucrats with their distrust of plain English call 'signage', and you and I call 'signs', sometimes tells us rather more than it intends. I am thinking particularly of a footpath sign that until recently stood droopingly at a hoop-gate on your left as you start the descent of Dancing Hill for Sherborne. It is one of a rash of the wretched things that infected our beautiful county at the millennium. Not only are they ugly, they are quite unnecessary: our precious rights-of-way were all admirably, and as near as possible permanently, marked by little disks screwed to gateposts and the like.

As well as being unsightly and otiose, the new signs are, most of them, dreadfully badly erected. Some eight feet long, they are sunk a totally inadequate fraction of their length into the ground. As I wrote at the time, and was publicly rebuked by a county councillor for so doing, 'No householder would pay an odd-job man for such sloppy work: a schoolgirl could have done it better.' The fruits of a make-work scheme thought up in an office by office people, they never had a hope of surviving the weather, let alone the rough and tumble of rural life. What this particular sign on Dancing Hill tells me every time I pass it is that a decade ago County Hall had nothing better to do with what they call 'resources', and we call 'cash', than waste it on fatuous and quite unnecessary 'signage'.

I don't much like notices, either. They seem to me to be a very poor way for country people to communicate with each other. All too often they insult the intelligence if not the manners of the reader. Bureaucrats love them, of course – nothing seems to please them more than bossing us around with fussy notices saying what we may or may not do.

Recently, however, I did myself put up a notice, although reluctantly. I was at my wits' end to know what to do about the poor wretched anorexic who daily dumped his/her uneaten, often shop-new and unopened 'rations' in the ditch at Dark's Bridge, no doubt going home to Mum and telling her how delicious they were. It was Diana's idea: she said as we rode by one morning, 'Why don't you put up a notice?'

Nailed lightly to a tree that stands there, it read, 'Would whoever leaves his/her uneaten food in the ditch please stop!? We try to keep our parish litter-free, and don't want to prosecute unless absolutely driven to it. So please, please stop.'

It worked. A few days later I took it down, apologising mentally to the tree and thinking regretful thoughts of the sad sandwich-flinger, whom I'd much rather help than curse. I thought of putting up a notice saying 'Thank you' but, as I say, I don't like notices, so I didn't.

* * *

Many of us surely know about horse mushrooms and rush to pick those delicious monsters before the maggots get the better of them. But few, I guess, will have heard of mushroom horses, or 'mushroom pointers' as they are often called: those mares – always mares, and always of working Irish stock – that sense the presence of, and are apparently irresistibly drawn to, mushrooms.

All 'pointers', and there are no more than a few hundred of them, go back to when the famous Irish Draft stallion, Big Orra, was put to the then champion laundry mare, Kilkenny Muffin, in 1922. Muffin was the first horse in which fungiphilia was noticed, and all pointers descend from the six fillies that she bred in the latter years of her life.

My mare Bella is one such. You would smile if you saw us,

apparently aimlessly tacking across the meadows on Dungeon Hill as she carries me from one clump of mushrooms to another. It's a great gift and I really value it, but it has a drawback, as I learned the hard way a few summers back.

Dorset's only polo club, at Orchard Portman, sadly folded in the wretchedly wet summer of 2007, when we just couldn't get

onto the ground to play. Before then, in answer to an SOS, I let them have Bella one afternoon for duty as an umpire's pony. It was a disaster.

If you have ever watched a game of polo, you will know that the shiny white ball, lying in grass, looks like nothing so much as a mushroom. The sight of what she took to be a mushroom zooming towards her quite unhinged poor Bella, who has not the steadiest of nerves at the best of times. She took off in the general direction of Sturminster Newton, carrying the hapless umpire over a five-bar gate and two enormous vale hedges before he could get her to answer to the bit. Luckily no harm was done, but it was a valuable lesson learned – and an appropriate story for the first day of this month of the year.

APRIL 2010

The Joys of the English Language

The special virtue of the old Dorset tongue is that it says what it means, words being like simple hand-tools, job-fit, time-worn, agelessly passed on, intended to reveal not conceal. I sometimes despair at what we do to our precious English language, it's a question of which I care for most, that or our countryside. The one has me forever off my horse picking up 'slob drops', as I call the litter that disfigures our lovely lanes, the other, you may well think, has me on a different horse – my high one – and one I don't intend to dismount.

From time to time a virus runs riot amongst the spoken word, putting plain English on life-support. For instance, do you remember basically, the time, some years ago, when people seemed to find it impossible to start on any topic without, basically, temporising with that so tiresome verbal tic? I was then a moderately large fish in a small pool, surrounded by people bent on pleasing me. I hung on the wall behind my desk, at eye-level to anyone on his feet addressing me, a legend that read 'Please do not use the word "basically" in this office'. It had a magic effect, rendering my interlocutors for a moment tongue-tied, forcing them actually to think about exactly what they wanted to say.

Today's equivalent must surely be the dreaded 'issue' virus. Listen to anybody being interviewed on the wireless and you might suppose that a rich prize was on offer for the most rapid and frequent use of that evasive weasel word, both interviewer and victim striving neck-and-neck to win. They mean, of course, to speak of problems, difficulties, worries and disagreements: so why on earth not simply say so?

Almost worse than the use of meaningless words and phrases is the inappropriate use of military jargon, of which surely 'friendly fire', as a means of alluding to the most tragic of battlefield blunders, must take the prize. Soldiers have always relied on irony to downplay the risk to which they expose themselves, but it is surely only the preserve of those who put themselves knowingly and willingly into harm's way to speak in this way.

Scarcely better than 'friendly fire' is 'Improvised Explosive Device', or 'IED', for 'mine' or 'roadside bomb'; don't blame the Army for this, they need their technical lingo, broadcasters do not.

'Call it the Home Guard,' said that greatest of Englishmen when his advisors were proposing all sorts of polysyllabic handles for what we today affectionately call 'Dad's Army'; how wise he was.

* * *

Aunts aren't what they used to be, if you'll forgive the pun, at least, since her regrettable divorce from 'Uncle Reith', 'Auntie Beeb' isn't the fine lady she was. Silly creature, a woman of independent means, having no need to curry favour with anyone, she long ago stopped teaching us grown-up behaviour and has joined us on the nursery floor, not to say in the gutter. But if, all too often, the BBC these days is a beacon of bad taste and imbecility, it is still, at its best, sublime, something to be really proud of. I both love and hate it.

The love affair goes back to my wartime childhood when our family, uprooted and fatherless for the duration, three small children and their brave young mother, crowded round the wireless at lunchtime and at six o'clock each evening, to hear the latest news, perhaps to hear that same great Englishman's peerless, lapidary, words, or, later, to laugh with Tommy Handley, hear Colonel Chinstrap say 'I don't mind if I do' and

Mona Lott the charlady ask 'Can I do you now sir?' in ITMA, 'It's That Man Again'.

I have the BBC to thank also for awakening me to music, long before I became a chorister and surrendered to music's formal but adored disciplines. It was a recording of *La Bohème*, on that same battered battery wireless; I can hear it now.

But what of my friend and almost constant companion the BBC today? Much of its output is anathema to me; waterboarding would be quite unnecessary if some enemy valued any secrets I might be supposed to own. They would just have to tie me up and make me listen to The Archers, or Any Questions, or put me out of reach of the on/off switch during the Today Programme. I'd spill the beans immediately.

But that's less than half the story. Thinking back to the turn of the year, do you remember that solid fortnight of Mozart, and the Sunday given over to the King James Bible? Did you feast, as I did, on the nightly readings from *Jamaica Inn*? For all its faults, I love the BBC, can't imagine life without it. Or as they say in Dorset, 'Wouldn't rightly know where I was to'.

APRIL 2011

Summer

Gerald, Tom & Mr Guppy

Memories were stirred the other day when I unearthed an old stable door from the out-shed where I, and my father before me, have for years stored wood that is too good to burn or throw away. I had completely forgotten about it and have no idea how long it had been stacked there: it was the top half-door of the forge, from when we had a shoeing smith in Glanvilles Wootton. I fancy I can hear my father say, 'If you've no use for that old door, Mr Guppy, I'll find a home for it' and the answer: 'You take 'n on Doctor, you're more 'n welcome to it.'

The old door had evidently served also as the village notice board, being pock-marked all over. Some of the drawing-pins

still survived, holding the corners of torn-down notices for who knows what long forgotten 'dos' in the Village Hall, church announcements, parish news, lost dogs and so on. What stories those marks could tell, if only the door could voice its memories – the approaching step, a notice goes up, neighbours read it, the event happens, more steps, and the notice comes down; over and over and over again . . . village life . . . falling leaves.

What was not fated to be forgotten, and stared me in the face when I got the old door onto my bench, was that the lower half was covered with names, burned into the wood. Mr Guppy evidently had a branding set for marking farm carts, tools and harness, and allowed the village boys to make free with it. H. Durden, H. Hounsell, B. Rose, C. Warren and others had left their marks there. And there was the name 'Dale', brothers, squire and parson here the best part of two centuries ago – the door cannot be that old, that must have been somebody's irreverent joke.

Mr Guppy, as I remember him in his old age, was not someone you would take liberties with. I must be the last person living who persuaded him, with many a grumble, to tighten a loose shoe, long after he had given up farrier's work. I was home from school one Christmas holidays and it saved me losing a precious day's hunting. I remember the old boy kindly for it, gruff, bitter-spoken and intimidating though he was.

He told me between hammer-blows of being gassed on Vimy Ridge with the Dorset Regiment. How I wish, oh how I wish, I had spent a bit of time with him, got him to talk more, coaxed them all out of him, written them all down, those precious, painful memories. What fools the young are to let such jewels slip through feckless fingers, never to be in their hands again, let alone held up to the light, pondered, studied, valued as they deserve. Is it nothing that Mr Guppy did for us, quitting family, home and safety, and going to that terrifying war: why had I not the wit and gratitude to learn more from him? We always leave it too late.

Old Tom, my father's groom/gardener, was another who had seen service with our county regiment on the Western Front. Tom was Dorset, generations deep, the last person whom I can remember speaking its language regularly to me and using no other.

My mother would have it that Tom was of gipsy extraction. Although he had settled kin around, he was himself rootless and roofless, having neither house nor wife as long as I knew him. Presenting himself for employment within days of our settling in Buckland Newton, the next village to here, in 1945, he lodged locally, shifting lodgings when we moved.

He attached himself to us; in a sense I think we were his family. I am ashamed to reflect that I did not like him better, was not more attentive and kind to him or take more notice of him when, old and worn out, he retired to the modern equivalent of the workhouse. I should have looked him up and made a fuss of him when I was home on leave.

One of the most telling stories of my mother's about Tom was of how she was talking to him one day as he dug the vegetable garden, when his fork turned up an old coin. 'In a twinkling,' my mother would say, 'sharp as that, he put his boot on it, thinking I hadn't seen it.' It tells you as much about my mother and her generation as it does about Tom that the coin ended up in her specimen cabinet.

How I wish that I had made more of old Tom, sat at his booted feet in the saddle room when he was having a brew-up at the coke stove, learnt all that he could have told me about his childhood, schooling and war service, of Thomas Hardy, whose birthplace he shared and whom he remembered well, and of now long-forgotten Dorset.

One always seems to leave it too late and, as I was reminded recently, in the tough farming world you may not have to go to war to be worthy of a medal. Gerald came to the parish first at Michaelmas in 1932, when he was five years old, his father having taken the tenancy of Church Farm, then part of the Castle Hill Estate. Little more than a month later his father was killed on the level-crossing in Sherborne. He was taking the milk in, as farmers did in those days, when the brakes on the lorry failed on Gas House Hill.

From that day, with just one older sister (who was to marry Mr Guppy's son) Gerald had to grow into being the man of the family. At the hand-inspection at the start of each day in our infant school the teacher used to say, 'We won't look at Gerald's hands; he's been milking.' So he had, and so he would be again after school, milking by hand of course. My next memory of him, by then a young man in his twenties, is his daily taking the churns down the drive for collection from the stand by Mr Guppy's forge.

When his mother died, Church Farm had to be sold by the Estate. Gerald, married by then, managed another farm in the parish. Early one morning, during milking, he was almost fatally trampled underfoot by a cow. On his own, with a fractured skull and smashed face, he somehow contrived to switch off the electricity and drive himself, not to the safety and care of his wife and home, just around the corner, but to Duntish, two miles off, so as to tell Stanley Mitchell how things stood in the milking parlour.

Only then did he summon help for himself. Stanley brought him to my father's surgery here and my mother, who had had a nurse's training, was, as always on such occasions, very much to the fore. An ambulance was summoned but three hospitals passed Gerald on, his case beyond them. Eventually he was expertly repaired and his skull riveted in Portland Naval Hospital. Imagine the travails and heroism of that young husband and wife that day, she following the ambulance by car!

That was almost the only time in seventy years of farming that Gerald troubled the doctors. 'He broke an arm once, and once had flu,' I was told, 'for a week.' Then, just after his eightieth birthday last Christmas, he took us all by surprise by dying. The last thing he did before he went to hospital was to plant out seventy-five young wallflowers, for he loved his garden.

* * *

The old door that I was telling of has found a use, as no doubt my father knew it would. It is set at eye-level in the wall of the shelter in our meadow, giving shade to the horses from the low evening sun when the flies are at their worst. It serves also as a memorial to those whose names are on it, a palimpsest of our village life through a century or more.

For me it is also a reminder of one particular 'Old Contemptible' who grumpily salvaged a day's hunting for the doctor's son one Christmas holidays so many years ago.

AUGUST 2008

Carnival Time

Films used once to be a great treat, especially during the war, but I can't have been inside a cinema more than three or four times in twenty or more years. Almost my first, certainly my most colourful, memory from childhood is of being taken to see Walt Disney's 'Snow White & the Seven Dwarfs'. The images, the ideas and the tunes from that wonderful film live with me still: 'Heigh Ho', 'Whistle While You Work', 'Some day my Prince will come' etc.

South Petherton, where we then lived, had an annual Carnival. Every year, with the help of my mother's dressmaker, we children were put into costume to take part in the parade. In

one particular year, I think it must have been 1938, my sister was Snow White, and my older brother and I dwarves. He was Happy and I – by my own choice, I would emphasise – was Dopey. Then, as now, yellow was my favourite colour, and Dopey, if you remember, wore a custard-coloured sort of nightdress, with a rather sweet droopy hat.

It was our most vocal blackbird, all too soon to moult and go silent, that put me in mind of Snow White and the way tunes linger in the memory. His favourite is a cascade of notes which I can't represent here, but it exactly mimics an often-repeated phrase in one of the songs in 'Mamma Mia', a charming film that one of our 'children' insisted on my watching, on video, during a recent trip to Italy. The 'mimic' in the case is of course not the blackbird, but Abba: well done them!

* * *

When I was a cadet at Sandhurst, we used to smile at an eccentric we called Camberley Kate, who kept a pack of miscellaneous dogs. It was a sight to see her walking them. We used to wonder what on earth her domestic arrangements could be and laugh at her, I hope not unkindly.

I think of Camberley Kate occasionally these days as people pass me, off my horse, picking up litter. I don't care what they think, but I do sometimes wonder. Just as Kate, providing a kindly home for strays, might possibly have thought herself the only sane person in a world of military maniacs, I take it as a compliment to be thought 'odd' in a world gone me-me mad.

I fancy that I can understand why people drop litter so shamelessly. We have a child-centred education system that majors on 'self-esteem'. It thus brings on succeeding generations of children who, poor deprived things, think first about themselves and grow up without properly becoming adults. It's all part of the 'nanny state': they throw stuff they don't want out of the pram.

Here in Glanvilles Wootton we have a scheme (guess who started it) whereby every stretch of road or lane in the parish is fostered, kept clean, by two or three families. We call them our 'pitches'. It works a treat. Litter breeds litter, as we all know, so the great principle is 'zero tolerance'. I will get down off my horse for as little as a sweet-paper and never go anywhere without a plastic bag in my pocket – preferably one of those orange ones from Sainsburys, so that people can see what I am doing.

Once or twice I have had the pleasure of returning litter to its source. One day, riding a favourite path up above Buckland Newton on Bladeley Hill, I found the contents of a whole house dumped. It was a terrible, pathetic sight: photograph albums, everything, the whole story of some family's life, once-loved things, strewn heartlessly under an indifferent sky.

It was a simple matter to trace the sad, on-the-move widow who had paid some wretch to dispose – as she supposed, legally – of what she could no longer house. It was just as simple to ring that wretch. One piece of advice: if you ever try this, disguise your number by dialling 141 before you dial his. They are fairly rough, some of these fly-tippers, and it is best if you yourself are not traceable.

This one was quite the hero on the telephone, telling me what he thought of me, but I could hear squabbling children and a pleading wife in the background, begging her man not to court trouble. I felt a twinge of compassion stirring and ended his bluster by saying, 'Don't worry, you'll hear no more of this as long as it is all gone by tomorrow.' It was.

JUNE 2009

The WI & Desert Island Discs

About this time last year the local branch of the WI, of which my mother had been for many years an active member, asked me if I would choose my 'Desert Island Discs' for public performance. I duly sent my selection, then forgot about it until I was reminded that the event was the next day by an apologetic telephone caller who asked if I would mind being my own interviewer, the neighbour detailed for the task having been whisked into hospital.

Wisely admonished not to 'cuff it' by a wife who has sat through too many of my halting deliveries – public speaking does not come easily, I find – I got up early and sorted out some questions to ask myself.

Apart from one sticky moment it seemed to go down quite well. In choosing my tunes all those months before, I had planned a ramble through my life, starting with my parents and ending in the beloved village where I grew up and to which I have returned to grow old.

My first choice, my father's favourite piece from opera, was, appropriately enough, although sung by a girl, 'O Mio Babbino Caro' or 'Oh My Beloved Daddy'; next came 'Amazing Grace'. Those present who remembered her appreciated the joke: everybody's neighbour, in later life my mother was known to one and all as Granny Grace.

School meant choir to me, so we had the 'Hallelujah Chorus'. Then came the sticky moment. I was describing what was for over thirty years my other family: my old regiment (the 13th/18th Royal Hussars) and the Army. Introducing 'Sunset and Evening Hymn', I was ambushed by my feelings and for a few awkward moments

found that I couldn't speak. I had wanted to say, as I recently heard a TA Bandmaster say so memorably in the Digby Hall, 'This is when we remember all those soldiers who, in past and present conflicts, never came home.' To this day I am not sure if I actually got the words out, before glancing rather desperately in the direction of my friend and neighbour who was manning the music machine. That was the one disc of my ten that we heard through from start to finish.

It was all plain sailing after that. 'Your Tiny Hand is Frozen', a nod in the direction of my passion for Italian opera, 'ridiculous stories set to heavenly music, fairy tales for grown-ups', as I describe it. 'Only You', sung by the Platters, was a concession to Diana, who said that my selection was too serious. The 'Posthorn Gallop' for our horses, Bach's 'Toccata and Fugue' for the church, our village church I mean, and then the wonderful bass aria from the last act of Tchaikovsky's *Eugene Onegin*, in which Prince Gremin tells his friend Onegin of the love and beauty brought into his life by marriage.

My final choice, yet more opera I'm afraid, was the drinking song that closes the first act of Verdi's *La Traviata*. If I had hoped that my kind audience might take a hint from this, I was to be disappointed, but a cup of coffee appeared. And then the treat of the evening: I was handed a CD with all my ten pieces on it. I play it endlessly.

* * *

'Goodbye, Delphie!' said a rather sad voice as I set out to transport our latest purchase away from her old home. Delphie is a very sweet-natured grey cob of Irish extraction. With her dumpy figure, big feet and Roman nose, perhaps the kindest description of her is *jolie laide*. But she is very well spoken of by people whom I trust (not always the case in horse-dealing) and I have every hope that she will, as our children say, 'do the business'.

'You must be mad! What on earth do you want with another horse?' an old regimental friend exclaimed. Mad indeed – with horses three's company, four's a crowd, you can lead three in hand, but never four, a fourth doubles the work – but the method behind the 'mad' purchase was to suit Diana with a horse she could trust and enjoy riding.

Some months back she had a catastrophic fall involving five separate fractures. She has already got back on skis and Delphie is to offer her a way back into the saddle, should she so choose; if not, the little mare will do for me. For the present my aim is to get her settled and going quietly in new surroundings. As I write we are daily getting to know and, I hope, to like each other; I certainly like her.

JULY 2009

Bella comes to Church

'Shall I?' . . . 'Dare I?' . . . 'What the Hell!' . . . While I was saddling Bella, my neighbour's son, Lee, had handed me the church key, reminding me that it was 'my' month again – six of us do two months each, the year round. I pocketed it and then, as we passed the churchyard wicket, found myself led into temptation. Why not sneak into the graveyard with Bella in tow to unlock that door, rather than leave the church shut until after my ride?

A nice piece of blacksmith's work, a memorial to a well-remembered squire, the gate was disfigured by two notices. One of them, almost covering the gate's crucifix, was an admonition to would-be thieves; the other was about dogs. How I hate such notices, fussy admonitions that are surely wasted on those for whom they are intended and are demeaning to the rest of us. But being reminded of what dogs were enjoined not to do on the consecrated ground did make me reflect on how much more seriously Bella might offend in that respect.

I led her gingerly through the wicket, praying that she would not lift her tail, climbed the winding path between where so many of my neighbours' forebears lie, sure at least that they, if they but could, would smile at our naughty trespass, and gained the porch.

Our church has a rather deep porch, with Ham-stone benches and a small ogee-headed window allowing a peep west to our garden wall. Even at the full length of her reins, it was necessary for Bella to half-enter so that I could slip the great key into the lock and turn its grudging mechanism. Was it, I wondered, the first time a horse had ever stood there?

What unpredictable animals horses can be! She, who would

jump a mile should a gnat unexpectedly clear its throat, seemed to be merely rather interested in the interior of the porch and its crowded notice-board. This was just as well as animals whose instinct leads them away from danger tend to discard excess baggage when nervous, but she behaved with perfect equanimity. I shall never forget the sight of her, ears cocked interrogatively, framed by that familiar Norman arch, the conduit over centuries past of so much joy and sorrow, so often the pulsing artery of our village life.

An oxymoron in stone, a locked church is anathema to me. What is the point of a church if you can't seek solace there at need, around the clock? If I had my way our church would be emptied of anything worth taking, so that the essential thing nobody can steal is always there, for everybody. To my mind the church's honour is at stake; as Shakespeare has Othello say, 'Who steals my purse steals trash.' Last year, when I was screwing up my courage to speak at a dear friend's memorial service in Dorset's 'cathedral', Sherborne Abbey, I went on from rehearsing there to visit the church where she worshipped as a girl, when we were both teenagers and I first knew her. I wanted to spend a little time in that place, on my knees. It was locked.

* * *

'Who's a clever boy then?!' I exclaim to the nymph at the tip, as I dutifully flatten all my cardboard before adding it to the mountain of stuff in the skip. 'Quite right,' she replies. 'Go to the top of the class!'

Sherborne's rubbish dump is not the least of its amenities. Such places self-select people with a social conscience and the old-fashioned manners that tend to go with one. Coming and going on its narrow lane, we readily make way for each other, exchanging salutes. As we con over the treasures displayed for sale, we smile sheepishly at each other, swap pleasantries. For not only is our tip an outpost of civilisation, it's a place to pick up bargains. Besides,

I bet not many rubbish dumps can boast a blonde.

The 'Canaletto' that hangs over my dressing-room mirror cost me 50p at the dump (actually it's a de Jongh and not an original, a gorgeous panorama of London and its bridge painted in 1660). The porter's trolley (remember railway porters?), indispensable to my outdoor labours, humping bales of hay and that sort of thing, cost me a similar sum.

I love gentle Sherborne: Cheap Street, the Abbey of course, Castleton's church, the schools with their music, the courteous shops, especially the charity shops that long ago usurped my London tailor, and Oliver's Coffee House where I go to read *The Times*. But on my way into town, I often take the turning at the foot of Dancing Hill that leads to the dump.

AUGUST 2009

Poems, Prose & Pandemonium

When I am doing outside jobs, I am often strongly reminded of the old men of the village, now long dead, who taught me the little I know about practical work out of doors.

John Guppy, our last blacksmith's son, came strongly to mind as I was cleaving a gatepost for firewood the other day. Goodness knows how long that post did duty at the entrance to our five-acre: it was given the *coup-de-grâce* by the baler when our hay was making last summer – and cost three times the making of the hay to replace!

Years ago, when it started to lean and the gate dragged on the ground, I set about trying to right it when John (Mr Guppy to me) came by and said something like 'Now young man, I'll show you how to do that job. You just go and find a good square wedge of stone.' And show me he did: first how to take the gate off its hinges, then free the post from the fence rails, next dig down on the outside of the post to make shift-room, then drive the stone wedge down on the inside until the post stood upright again – as it did for I don't know how many years until the baler's fatal nudge. There's nothing like oak!

As I cleft the stubborn old post, I fell to wondering who taught John to right a gatepost, who taught his tutor, who taught him, and so on? It was a good feeling, being part of such a lineage. Let's hope I have a chance to pass the inheritance on.

Jim Ross, again not ever so called by me, taught me never to leave the stump in the ground when you fell a tree or clear a casualty, and showed me how this most muscular of jobs is best done. Jim, who had been a linesman for BT and gardened for my parents on retirement, also taught me fencing: how to get the wire really taut, and a dozen other things.

We did a lot together, Mr Ross and I. When he died, his widow, Doris, gave me his small pocket winch, which has a thousand uses and is one of my most treasured implements. Mrs Ross worked indoors for my mother almost from the first day we arrived here. There was no doubt some formality in those far-off times, but they became the best of friends and inseparable in old age, their daily joy being puzzling over *The Daily Telegraph* crossword – we won't say which one! Sadly, Mrs Ross has now followed her old friend to the grave. We all miss her.

I can't remember who taught me always to look out for heavily pregnant ewes trapped on their backs, and how to right them. One morning last January, when I went to get the horses in for work, they were standing as if electrified, staring out of the paddock in the direction of the manor. Horses can be rather dangerous in such a mood; they don't mean to knock you down and trample you, but it can all too easily happen. 'Horseplay' is indeed rough. Bella was too distracted to be caught, but dear Delphie quietly exchanged her freedom for a piece of apple. As I led her in, I spotted the cause of the fracas. A ewe was on her back, kicking furiously, just across our boundary hedge. It was a matter of minutes to right her and to see her scamper gratefully off.

* * *

Our 'Village Entertainment' back in February was such fun that it is still fresh in my mind. It was an evening of 'Poems, Prose & Pandemonium' in the Village Hall. My part, which featured in the programme as 'Mystery Item', involved my slouching in, grunting aggressively, with a can in my hand and wearing a 'hoodie' and scruffy old pair of over-trousers that Delphie and I had picked up, discarded by the roadside, a few weeks before.

Once on the stage I unveiled, and gave my neighbours in rough verse, a brief account of what I call the 'Dark's Bridge

Mystery', which I have written about here – how some poor wretched anorexic for some weeks dumped unwanted, unopened supermarket food items in the ditch there, and how we put a stop to it. I have learnt over the years that you can get away

with spouting almost any old rubbish if you make it rhyme.

What I can never forget of those evenings – we played a Friday and Saturday, to full houses – is waiting outside the hall's fire exit as the pianist played Beethoven's Für Elise: one of the first pieces I more or less mastered as a schoolboy, and once myself played in a concert. The applause dying was my cue to knock on the door and gruffly demand admittance. The connection between those two nervous moments in my life, separated as they were by well over sixty years, seemed very telling.

But more memorable for me even than that was the happy hubbub in the hall at the interval and at the end, as neighbours chatted and their children, in Oliver Twist costumes, swarmed amongst us. Several times I shut my eyes, just to drink in the sound, and thought, 'Why can't the whole world live in amity like this?' I felt so proud of our little village, so grateful that we live there.

JUNE 2010

War Horse

I am sure that we are not the only happily married couple to be a little careful about sharing plans and information, to practise a bit of judicious domestic 'news management', careful timing so often being essential to a successful *dénouement*.

For instance, when we got back from skiing last Easter, I was dismayed to notice that the electric 'fencer', quite an expensive item, was missing from its place in a corner of our meadow. Nor was it on my work-bench, whither I had a vague memory of shifting it for safety, nor anywhere in our outbuildings where I might absent-mindedly have stowed it.

The first few days after coming home are always rather fraught, with everything to do and no time to do it, so, having covertly priced a replacement, I chose my moment carefully to break the news of the loss, mentioning it casually on about day seven while we were out riding. 'Oh, I hid the fencer in your mother's old pantry. I didn't think it was safe on your bench' was the comforting reply!

The boot was on the other foot when I had to pretend that I knew nothing in advance about my surprise birthday treat. Diana, who is so careful to make all diary entries in shorthand so that she can tell me what I need to know when I need to know it, can be forgetful of 'security' when on the telephone. Hence I overheard the word 'warhorse' some four weeks before the family gave me the happiest birthday I can remember, and in London of all unlikely places – I never go east of Salisbury unless duty calls.

What can I tell you that you don't already know of *War*

Horse, the long-running play at the National Theatre about a West Country-bred horse that saw front-line service in the First World War? I think the biggest surprise was the breadth of its appeal. Not only, evidently, does it 'speak' powerfully to the non-horsey majority, but my step-grandchildren, almost teenage down to tinies, loved it as much as I did.

* * *

You wouldn't believe the hullabaloo Bella made when we left her on her own one morning. It's a thing I never normally do, for fear she will injure herself rushing around heedlessly, not to mention waking all our neighbours – it was a Sunday morning. But she was being silly about being caught for work, so on a whim I said, 'I'll take your brother, that'll teach you!'

I hadn't been on Dandy's back since my 75th birthday, over two years ago, when I sadly concluded that his working days were over, and that before we got into another winter of expensive feeding he would have to 'go on'. But I could never find the heart to follow up and had anyway sort of half-promised myself and them that brother and sister would see out their days together.

Dandy took the whole once-so-familiar routine in his stride – horses forget nothing, I am convinced of that – and walked off boldly and quietly from the mounting block as if he had been doing it every day all these past months. It was such a pleasure to be on his back again, to find him moving freely, trotting sound; he had been chronically lame from our last, catastrophic fall, when I retired him.

As we left the village, the Rector and then the organist passed us on the road. That was an embarrassment because we had a busy day ahead – lunch out and, for me, an afternoon full of work at Melbury's puppy show – so I had intended to skip church, but this encounter made that impossible.

Not pushing our luck with Dandy, we rode just a mile out of the village to Dark's Bridge and back. We dropped the horses in their meadow, Chantry Mead, and I sprinted up the lane to church, much to the amusement of a group from Sherborne Girls School, who were on a hike and had been comforting bereft Bella over her gate. I got in as the first lesson was being read, creeping into a back pew.

Of course I didn't have my reading glasses with me and the hymns were a bit of a trial – you think the words are familiar enough, but when it comes to singing them full voice, you suddenly find you don't. The warden in the pew in front of me, an old friend, intimated that I was a verse out, or perhaps even singing the wrong hymn at one stage. And then of course I had nothing for the collection but the quarter-apple that should have been Dandy's. That was declined, but raised a smile.

Everyone took my little *jeu d'esprit* in good part. 'Where's your horse?' asked the Rector, seeing the saddle, bridle, whip and hat stacked in the porch. The upshot is that I am going to take Dandy back into gentle work again.

AUGUST 2010

Talking French to Bella

'Behavez-vous votre self, s'il vous plaît!' I say to naughty Bella, as I try to struggle her into her bridle. It's like trying to put on an eel's socks; she fights the whole way, always, and always does her best to remove one of my fingers as she at last accepts the bit between rebellious teeth. She's a dear, Bella, I adore her – mad as the proverbial hatter, typical chestnut mare, but quite the sparkiest, most responsive and rewarding hack I've ever sat on.

She is also highly intelligent, and brilliantly helpful when I am opening and shutting field gates, the mechanics of which she mastered as a two-year-old, when we first put her under the saddle sixteen years ago. Bella doesn't speak foreign languages of course, but understands the tone of voice. Italian does just as well, particularly the explosive 'Basta!', meaning 'Enough!', which I find works with children too.

I was, as you may have guessed, perfecting my mastery of the French language as I saddled her up for a last ride before a trip across, or rather under, the Channel. You should have seen the fuss when we presented ourselves and our luggage for inspection, before boarding the Eurostar at Waterloo. Just as we were leaving home, a call from our hosts had advised bringing extra warm clothing, so I switched a smart top-coat for my stables jacket . . . which of course has a clasp-knife in one pocket, for broaching hay bales.

Got there? Mayhem erupted when the knife showed up on the x-ray machine, there was such excitement amongst officialdom we must have made their day. I have been told since, by less fortunate travellers, that I was lucky not to have the offending weapon, which is very dear to me, an heirloom, permanently confiscated. As it was, it was returned to me, on the quiet, by a very pleasant young lady, along with a gently smiling rebuke, she saying that I was breaking the law by carrying such a thing about my person. I always think of her now as I use it, grateful that she had a sense of humour and could turn a blind eye to a daft law: I wish that there were more like her.

* * *

It was on our return from the continent that my new friend Cocky first showed up. He would meet me at the paddock gate first thing as I went to get the horses from Chantry Mead, the meadow across the lane, onto their day-pasture and for their breakfast. He would help himself from one of their feed-bowls, cheeky thing, while I fetched them . . . or rather, as they fetched themselves; I just open the gates, they know the drill.

Sometimes Cocky would vary the routine by following me, at heel, like a dog, just to check out the horses' tea-site, in case he had overlooked any pickings on the previous afternoon. I never actually touched him, but he became extraordinarily tame and trusting . . . and vocal, making endearing little, happy-sounding, approving, liquid clucks as he pecked around my feet. Sometimes he would crow and clap his wings, there, just by me.

I could never get used to the extravagant beauty and variety of his plumage. A healthy live cock-pheasant, his ancestors immigrants from the Black Sea shore a thousand years or more back, just radiates exotic magnetism, and, in my mind at least, raises all sorts of unanswerable questions. How could such superfluous, detailed, aesthetic splendour, so pleasing to the human eye, just have evolved by chance, or in response to picky preferences expressed over millennia by the dowdy female of the species? Surely some Designer took a hand? I just don't understand, but am inclined to credit Creation rather than Natural Selection . . . a shocking thing for someone who bears the name Gould to say. My Dorset-born great-great-grandfather, is credited with giving Darwin his eureka moment, by suggesting an explanation of the variations in the finches he had brought home in HMS *Beagle*.

On the morning of writing this I rode the bridle-path that runs the edge of Middlemarsh Common, hoping to see progeny of the even more splendid golden pheasant that I found living there ten years or so ago, and which, like Cocky, used to follow my horse's heels, almost the length of the wood, clucking; he must have been somebody's pet. Sadly, there was no trace of him.

When, with the new grass coming strongly through, we left off the winter feeding routine, Cocky went AWOL too. It had nothing to do with the shooting season, by then long over, he had evidently found another friend. It was a case, I must suppose, of *cherchez la femme*.

JUNE 2011

The Hedgerow Elm

As you leave Glanvilles Wootton, heading south for Buckland Newton, a massive oak leans over the road, in blessing and farewell to the traveller I like to think. It is, no doubt, a descendent of one of the great trees of the Forest of Blackmore, to which our village in part owes its name.

A few paces on, across the road, on the boundary of our land, standing over a stile, an ancient way-mark on the route for outlying parishioners across Chantry Mead to church, is my favourite ash, my seasonal weather-forecaster. Unusually late in leaf this year, it told us all about the weather we are enjoying, or suffering, as you read this.

Both those trees owe their longevity, and their shape, to the fact that, as youngsters, they were pollarded. That is to say that they were 'girt', their trunks cut clean through, usually at about ten feet from the ground, a height that rendered the subsequent outgrowth of succulent young branches safe from the attentions of browsing deer and cattle. The woodman would re-visit at intervals to harvest the crop of valuable fire and fencing timber.

This practice all but died out in the late eighteenth century, the trees subsequently growing out to develop the familiar 'cabbage' shape that they have today. That they survive so well – think of those massive oaks in Windsor Great Park – is thanks to their low centre of gravity, which saves them from being maimed or felled by high winds, and the fact that they generally hollow out, a cylinder being so light and strong, not to mention being unattractive to the timber merchant!

I find that not everybody knows about pollarding, and the part it has played in shaping the character of our countryside

. . . just about all our really old hardwood trees are pollards. I was certainly completely ignorant on the subject until, some thirty years ago, Oliver Rackham's *The History of the Countryside* came into my hands; it's a wonderful book that I cannot too strongly recommend. It has been such a help to me in trying to read below the surface of the bit of Dorset where I have grown up and which I have come so to love.

I dare say that the name just mentioned will have made some

of the older amongst you think of *Sleepy Hollow*, a book we had as children, illustrated by Arthur Rackham (1867-1939). No connection I believe, but what a strong echo when one thinks of characterful trees!

Passing 'The Three Elms' public house in North Wootton the other day put me in mind of what a feature hedgerow elms used to be in the Dorset of my boyhood, before that awful Dutch Elm Disease bereaved us of them. On Dungeon Hill this morning, I was reminded of how the view across the Blackmore Vale has changed since I first knew it. Then, it was almost like looking across a forest, not to say a battlefield, every small field ringed with tall mushroom clouds of foliage.

Today the view from Dungeon is differently splendid. West you can see to Exmoor possibly, the Brendons for sure, south the skyline is the Dorset Heights with their storied ridgeway, east to Bulbarrow marking the edge of Cranborne Chase and, to the north, reminders of two kings: one of history, one of legend.

A neighbour recently boasted to me of how she could see Arthur's Seat from her garden – that would indeed be a view to be proud of, all the way to Edinburgh – we had a good laugh about it. She meant Alfred's Tower of course, almost always in view from Dungeon. But, on a clear day, you can also make out Arthurian reminders in the shape of Glastonbury Tor, and Cadbury Castle.

The ride home took Delphie and me through Park, the field above our Manor House, and past two favourite old trees. One, an incredibly tortured ash of great age, its short hollow trunk, its bolling (long 'o') to use the woodman's term, split from crown to turf, its whole mien suggesting agony. The other an even older oak, hollow again, but with a toothless mouth that seems to howl at me in predatory rage, its up-raised branches talons ready to pounce.

Sleepy Hollow indeed! How we children loved that book, in which Arthur Rackham's trees somehow suggested nightmare but sent us smiling to our beds.

AUGUST 2011

Autumn

Holy Smoke

This old house has been my home since we moved here from Buckland Newton when I was a schoolboy. It has a Georgian front, to which visitors seldom find their way, stuck at right angles on a Tudor long house. Perhaps its most special feature is a kitchen courtyard, through which all callers, from Toffee the gamekeeper's cat to the Lord Lieutenant, reach our back door. With its straggle of outbuildings, stables and so on, stretching back from the long house, seen from the air the place must look like a letter 'P'.

One of the advantages of living in what used to be a rectory is that you know just who lived there in the past and when. In our case we have only to go down the orchard path to the church and study the roll of rectors. It opens with one John Sprot, who was first appointed 706 years ago, long before any part of this house was built. I often find myself wondering what the Reverend Mr Sprot was like.

But we have a special, very specific reminder of one pair of rectors, John Woodman, father and son, who had the living from 1857 to 1881. The heights and ages of some of the Woodman children are recorded in pencil behind a bedroom window shutter. The writing looks as though it was done yesterday.

When a great-niece of mine recently visited from Australia, she slept in that room. It was once upon a time her grandmother's, and before that my grandmother's. That's five generations: I really begin to feel that we can claim to belong in Glanvilles Wootton.

* * *

Ours is a dear little church on the edge of the village, in the middle of the fields almost. No doubt there are a thousand and more village churches just like it across the land, but for me it has no rivals – I suppose that's what being 'parochial' means. It's so full of memories.

Just by the font, on the right as you go in, is a wall plaque to my father. We were lucky to get permission for it, the last one granted before the authorities put a stop to such memorials. It describes him as 'a loved family doctor', which is no more than the truth. It is more than forty years since he was stolen from us by the usual thief, at a tragically early age, but he is still remembered. Just a few weeks ago, as we were leaving a local party, a reveller's voice called out, 'Good night, Doctor!' – people say that I am the spitting image of him.

We nearly lost our church recently. It was the last Sunday of last year, the Feast of the Holy Innocents. My wife, Diana, was taking an early walk and chanced, if it was chance, to look in on the church, 'to check the Christmas flower arrangements,' she said. Opening the door, she was met by a wall of smoke.

Four fire engines arrived with commendable alacrity. One of

the crewmen told us that, with any delay, the whole precious building would have gone. As it was, we lost a few old pews and the place was unusable for stink and grime. Faulty wiring was the cause. The village rallied round, as it always does, but it was not until the middle of last month that we were able to hold a service there again. You would be surprised – or perhaps you wouldn't – how many important people crept out of the bureaucratic woodwork, crying, 'Hang on, wait for us!'

* * *

While everybody else was worrying about the church on that hectic morning, we were in a panic about our horses. One of them, Diana's pony, Harvey, was on 'box rest' following a knee operation and at all costs he needed to be kept quiet. Horses are easily frightened into violence, so for weeks 'Do Not Disturb' had been the rule in our stable yard.

All too frequently people mistake our drive for the road to the church: the thought of a fire engine clanging and clattering its way up there was terrifying. I rushed down to prevent it.

It was a strange feeling that winter morning, one I shall never forget, waiting for the wail of the engines to snake in to the village from the distant main road. It reminded me of another Sunday morning, a year or so ago, when my ears strained for the sound of an approaching helicopter . . . But that's a story for another day.

SEPTEMBER 2008

Saved by Air Ambulance

'I have lived here since August 28th, 1951' reads a note in a familiar hand, recently found at the back of a drawer. My mother was in her early forties when we came here, a tough war behind her, moving the whole time, bombed out once, my father at sea. Seventeen years of married life and nearly twice that of widowhood lay ahead of her that summer half a century ago until, on a hateful day, I had to take her from the home she loved. I can never forget nor cease to regret that journey, although truly we had no choice but to put her in professional hands for the last few weeks of her life.

Born, like Nelson, in the parsonage at Burnham Thorpe in Norfolk, she was a woman of character, very much of her generation. She never really gave up being 'the doctor's wife'; almost to the end she was, you might say, a neighbour-at-large to the village. Not for nothing is she the central figure in our millennium photograph. Not for nothing is she still kindly spoken of by one and all as Granny Grace.

* * *

When we came here on that August day over fifty years ago and this village lost its parson, at least it gained a doctor. Back then we had two pubs, a school, post office, chapel as well as church, and a farrier not yet totally retired. More than a dozen herds were milked in the parish and the first job each morning for one of us children when we were on holiday from school was to walk down to Manor Farm with the milk can.

Now all but the church and one single herd are gone. The Post

Office was closed several years ago, outrageously; it was done almost overnight by distant, high-handed officialdom. 'You'd think we lived in Russia,' my 90-year-old mother said, suddenly robbed of one of the pleasures of her week, walking down the village to collect her pension.

* * *

Last month I wrote of how we nearly lost our church, too, last Christmas and of how waiting for the fire engines had reminded me of straining my ears for the sound of an approaching helicopter on another winter Sunday morning a couple of years earlier.

A neighbour had beguiled me. Instead of going to church, I accepted a lift in her lorry for a ride on the downs above Sydling St Nicholas. God is not to be mocked – my old horse, Dandy, put both front feet into a rabbit hole when we were cantering a headland, did a cartwheel and landed squarely on top of me.

I was completely trapped, luckily under the smooth of his broad shoulder, clear of the saddle. I could so easily have been killed outright but in fact, at the time, had no pain. The situation seemed comic more than anything, except that Dandy was motionless, a dead weight. I thought that he had broken his back. 'Come on, Dandikins, stir yourself!' I said into his nearest ear. I couldn't bear the thought that my old friend of so many years was dead; he was born in our paddock.

Luckily again, he paid no attention, for when he did recover from being merely winded, his wild struggles to regain his mailed feet must surely have done for me. My riding companion had pulled me clear by then. While Dandy wandered quietly off to graze, I lay in the sun, unable to stand. I enjoyed the accusing sound of Sydling's church bells and listened for that helicopter.

Dandy was never quite the same horse again and he is now retired. I found myself out of the saddle for five long months while my pelvis mended. My only lasting injury is a muscular tic that has my hand diving into my pocket whenever I see a Dorset Air Ambulance collecting tin.

* * *

October, more than any other month, is the time when atavistic superstitions surface – Hallowe'en and all that. I have no time for such feeble-mindedness. As long as you always 'touch wood', are careful not to walk under ladders, do the right thing with spilt salt, and take sensible precautions should you see a single magpie, what is there to worry about?

I do however have one golden rule: I try never to quit the house without a hoof-pick, toothpick, penknife and length of binder-twine about my person. Forgetting this on a recent, rare, reluctant trip to London got me into a dreadful scrape. More of that another day . . . (*see* 'Talking French to Bella').

OCTOBER 2008

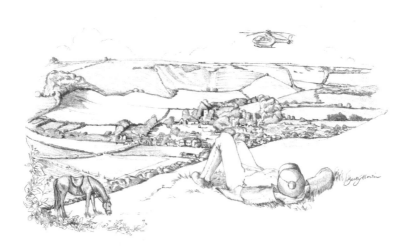

Randy & Doris

Although I was never a Boy Scout, Lord Baden-Powell stood at my shoulder throughout the most crucial juncture of my life. It happened like this. When I first joined my old regiment there was an oil painting of the great man in our mess room. He had served with us and we were proud of it. Exploring the Mess later, I found another portrait, neglected, in a back corridor: a crayon sketch by Augustus John.

When some twenty years on I found myself commanding my beloved regiment, I had that picture moved to my office. Thus for three years I had a daily reminder of the Hero of Mafeking, that Brownsea Island pioneer, and his deathless motto, 'Be prepared!'. There was therefore no excuse whatever for my going to London one day last May without the customary hank of binder-twine in my pocket.

A favourite niece, who is an Army vet, had been rewarded on return from a tour with the war dogs in Iraq by being appointed to the King's Troop Royal Horse Artillery. She invited us up to St John's Wood as guests of the Troop for the State Opening of Parliament.

Luckily I at least had the wit to go properly dressed, as, after a magic morning amongst all the congenial noise and bustle of six gun-teams and the best part of seventy horses being fettled up, the senior officer present turned to me and said 'Got your hat? . . . Stand there!' I was to take the salute as the guns left barracks to cross London for their royal duties! The Army never really lets you go: once a soldier, always a soldier. I could not have dreamed of such an honour coming my way and it all but brings a tear to my eye to write of it.

Unfortunately, no doubt due to the swelling of my chest, some time during that proud, unforgettable morning my braces snapped, so that I was obliged to acknowledge the salutes of the returning gun teams with one hand managing my bowler hat, the other at my waist-band.

* * *

Does anybody read, or even remember, Ernest Thompson Seton (1860-1946) nowadays? He was a Canadian born, and in part educated, in this country, who wrote the most wonderful 'animal biographies': *Lives of the Hunted* and *Animals I Have Known* are two of the titles that remain in my head. I can't find any of his books about the house, so my sister must have snaffled them. They were about the wild animals of Canada, wolves mainly, and we adored them.

From Ernest Thompson Seton I learnt the pleasure of trying to identify individual wild creatures, give them names, look out for them, follow their fortunes, share their lives.

It isn't often possible, but when it is, it's a joy.

A year or so ago there was a roebuck that I named Randy, resident in nearby Hay Wood. During the rut, whenever I approached the margins of his territory on the massive chestnut horse I had then, Randy would bark a challenge at us from the depth of the wood. There is surely no more feral sound than a roe's bark, not in these islands anyway. Once, when we met him head-on in a ride in his wood, he stood his ground, stamped his foot and looked as if to charge us before making off with his mate, Doris. I suspect that she, having the normal timidity of her species, did not approve of such a brazen way of carrying on.

Birds offer an easier study for the would-be biographer. For well over a year now my life has been coloured by a robin called Henty. Until the moult he had a white feather in his wing (*White Feather* by G.A. Henty – get it?). Summer and winter, morning and evening, Henty greets me with his song as I walk through the shrubbery to see our horses. If I work in that part of the garden he immediately joins me, is almost at my feet in his keenness to forage where I have disturbed the ground.

Last summer, during a precious time when we had all our children and grandchildren staying with us, I was sitting at the front doorstep early one morning before the house awoke. Henty flew down from busying himself in the wisteria and perched for a never-to-be-forgotten fragment of a second on my shoulder before fluttering on down to hunt for whatever robins hunt for on the lawn.

NOVEMBER 2008

Grabbing the Queen's Flowers

Looking back on the summer just past, as one tends to at this time of year, one event stands out: the privilege of having luncheon with Her Majesty The Queen at St James's Palace. The occasion was the 500th anniversary of the founding of the Queen's Bodyguard, the Honourable Corps of Gentlemen at Arms, by King Henry VIII; I have been invited to write their commemorative history, hence the invitation.

Our great day started in the Chapel Royal. A memorable service, with wonderful music, was followed by a parade in one of the Palace's courts. Then we trooped upstairs to the State Apartments for a reception, all to be in turn presented to Her Majesty.

I hope that I have not given the impression that our luncheon was *tête-à-tête*; there were in fact some two hundred of us. When the party broke up and the Queen and Prince Philip had left, word circulated that all the flower arrangements were going to be binned by the caterers and that we guests might, if we so pleased, help ourselves. Seizing the moment, I grabbed the biggest arrangement of them all, the one in the centre of the Queen's table.

Picture me if you can, clasping it to my chest on the Tube from Green Park as rush hour built. Then it proudly decorated the table in our railway carriage all the way down to Sherborne. A single, barely-open rose I gave to the Jamaican lady in the left-luggage store at Waterloo Station, who had shown, and so prettily, an interest in the great event of our never-to-be-forgotten day, which she had somehow got to know of. The rest of the arrangement spent the following Saturday in the church, an object of great interest and admiration at our fête.

* * *

A few Sundays later, I found myself sitting in the garden, watching and listening to the birds as I waited to go to church. I was in a grump. Our hay, for the first time I can remember, was lying rotting in the paddock thanks to a monsoon of thunderous rain. Having gone to bed late and risen languid, we had foregone our morning ride. Worst of all, my best friend – what I still think of as the BBC's 'Home Service', nearly always to be relied upon to talk sensibly to me about what is going on in the wider world – was having one of its occasional fits of infantilism. It rabbited on obsessively, going on and on and on about an event which no intelligent grown-up person could possibly be interested in, let alone wish to dwell upon in any detail.

Church put me into a better frame of mind. It was Communion and I was to read the Gospel. Greatly daring, Diana having put me up to it, I begged the congregation's indulgence when I got to the lectern and prefaced the reading by saying that the tie that I was wearing was that of my old regiment, currently in Afghanistan for the third time, and that I wore it in their honour to mark Armed Forces Day.

The Gospel itself was not an easy read. A favourite passage but very long – twenty-two verses from Mark V – it tells the story of two healing miracles. First, Jairus, 'one of the rulers of the synagogue, fell at his feet, and besought him greatly saying my little daughter lyeth at the point of death.' Then we learn of the woman who, as Jesus made his way to Jairus's house, touched his garment and was healed.

In one of the Bible's rare uses of the original Aramaic, Our Lord says to the twelve-year-old girl, 'Talitha cumi'– 'Damsel, I say unto thee, arise.' The passage ends with him 'commanding that something should be given her to eat'. It is all so beautifully expressed, so immediate, so simple, with such perfect use of our

so precious language, that I found it quite difficult not to get lost in the feelings it evoked and actually to give level voice to the words. However, by getting a grip, I got away with it.

As we left, with the usual handshaking in what I now think of as Bella's porch, the Rector thanked me not only for reading but for mentioning my regiment. I thanked him for not mentioning Michael Jackson.

SEPTEMBER 2009

Army Life

Like soldiers, horses spend a great deal of their lives waiting for whatever is due to happen to them next, and no doubt muttering to themselves the equine equivalent of 'What the **** is that ****ing officer doing!? Where is he? Where's our grub?'

Don't get me wrong. Soldiers are great masters of irony: it makes a tough life bearable. There is boundless mutual respect between the ranks of a good regiment and it wouldn't work any other way. Soldiers know that their welfare, in the broadest sense, is the first and last concern of their officers. 'See to the horses first, next the men, only then you can go to the Mess' was the rule in old cavalry regiments and in spirit it still holds.

When I was a cadet at Sandhurst my Company Commander was a war hero with a DSO. The late David Owen, gently spoken, slow to smile, was and still is my beau ideal of an Army officer. When one of us bright young things had given voice to some brilliant military plan in answer to a problem set us, he would ask ever so quietly, 'What about the men's tea-meal?' It is a quaint locution which, as you can see, did its work and has stayed with me. Perhaps one of the proudest moments of my young life was when, towards the end of my middle term at Sandhurst, Major Owen sought me out and said, 'I want you to be my Senior Under Officer next term.'

* * *

Rather like success at school, though, success at Sandhurst as often as not does not imply a meteoric later career. Being quite unsuited to the Army, I was lucky to get where I did. But it is the special genius of a British regiment – especially, as I like to think, of a line cavalry regiment – to fit oddities in, make use of their talents and cover for their failings.

Will you believe me when I tell you that I managed to rise to command of an armoured regiment, and survive it, without having the faintest idea – or wishing to have the faintest idea – of how a tank functions? I loathed the beastly things, their smells and sudden noises. As long as I could count to 45, which was the number of the brutes we were required to field, there were plenty of loyal friends around me to take care of the technical side and keep the tracks rolling.

What I did reckon to understand was that the health, effectiveness and reputation of a regiment rests, more than on any other single factor, on the quality of the young officers it is able to attract and to retain. I saw it as my job to make sure that their life was generally attractive, the serious side balanced by fun.

The thought was brought strongly home to me in July when I found myself writing up the annual polo match between the Army and the Royal Navy for *Horse & Hound*. All the players wore black armbands; it was the day after the loss of eight of our soldiers in Afghanistan. It can seldom have been more important than it is now to keep the lighter side of service life going, so that when my old regiment returns from its third tour in that benighted country this month, they can pick up where they left off.

As I write, already all too many Light Dragoons have come home via Wootton Bassett. I pray, literally, that no more return that way.

* * *

'WHAT have you done with the Lawrences catalogue?' Diana demanded, as we met one morning by chance, she walking the neighbour's dog, me exercising her new horse, Delphie, or

'Goody-four-shoes' as I have come to call her.

'I threw it away. The sale was last week, wasn't it?'

'But I wanted to find out what one of the lots went for.'

Gloom . . . I'm always in trouble for prematurely throwing things away. There was nothing for it, when I had turned Delphie away to graze, but to grab the saddle-room stool, leg it down to the Village Hall, climb into the skip and search for the wretched thing. Needless to say, I had not been the last of our neighbours there. In fact it was interesting leafing through, guessing who had left what. I was quite tempted to extract one or two engaging-looking periodicals, but didn't and merely pounced with relief and delight on what I was looking for, which I found several strata down. My reward was an accolade that between husband and wife surely cannot be bettered. 'You are sweet!' my adored wife of thirty years said.

OCTOBER 2009

Digging for Victory

Not the least of the small pleasures of what I call the 'Brownturn' are echoes of the provident practices learnt in a wartime childhood, for instance re-using envelopes and now teabags. Best of all, though, is 'Digging for Victory'. I love my vegetable garden, not least because everything in it does more or less what it's told, or seems to try to, and stands in straight lines.

Apart from making music, is there anything in life more blame-free than growing vegetables? It was a bumper year, with virtually no watering necessary. The slavery of a record strawberry crop – do you remember how Jane Austen describes the galloping ennui of picking strawberries in *Emma*? – gave way to the tyranny of the heaviest bean-harvest I can recall. Those wretched beans, with their brilliant camouflage: however diligently you search for them, a few always evade capture and grow too large to eat.

Beet, courgettes, cauliflower, celeriac, a battalion of leeks, onions we had in profusion; herbs, of course, and what old Tom used to call 'lady's flowers', that is flowers for the house. But carrots won't grow for me for some reason. I try not to grow potatoes, however tempting their generous harvest, because they will leave small insubordinate stragglers that go AWOL, then pop up untidily in unwanted places in subsequent years.

The only failure I had this year was with my maize. This led me into a scrape of which I am thoroughly ashamed and of which, if I confess it on this page, I hope I may be shriven. Just one, and only one, of the twenty cob-seeds I planted germinated. Maize has to mate so, out riding one day, the naughty thought

71

struck me that a couple or so of the countless thousand young plants standing in a nearby field would make companions for my poor solitary and would not be missed. Next time out, I took a trowel and a saddlebag and did the deed.

If you are smiling, perhaps it is because you know what I did not, but in due course discovered: that maize grown for cattle is unpalatable to humans. God is not mocked.

A scrape of quite a different sort had me truly frightened a short while back. Riding Delphie one Sunday morning before church, just a quick out-and-home to Dark's Bridge at Round Chimneys (a favourite, storied, historic spot), I was disgusted to find that someone had dumped a whole load of household rubbish on the verge and in the cavernous ditch that feeds the un-named stream nearby.

I picked up what I could reach and Delphie could carry, and

later that day, still fuming in a most un-Christian way, banged off an e-mail to the address at Nordon where you report such things. A week and several exchanges later, I was told that the area had been cleared and was asked to confirm that the 'Street Cleaning Supervisor' had in fact visited the right spot.

He had, but he hadn't made a very good job of cleaning it up. A yoghurt carton and a crisp packet lay in full view, with more leftovers in the bottom of the ditch. While 'Goody Four Shoes', as I call saintly Delphie, diligently grazed the verge at the extent of her reins, I scrambled down into the ditch and cleared it.

When I came to try to climb out, I realised what a foolish thing I had done and what a pickle I was in. I couldn't readily get a foothold on the greasy ditch face to climb out. It was nearly six feet deep and Delphie's mailed feet were at my eye-level. Had she taken fright, I wouldn't have had a chance of holding on to her. Her breaking free from my tenuous grasp of the rein buckle and galloping the road home didn't bear thinking about.

Somehow, by getting a firm grasp of a tussock in the verge and kicking toeholds in the bank face, I eventually clambered out, chastened. I shan't do that again.

NOVEMBER 2009

Snowdrop Corner & Dorset Byways

I was a young man in my early twenties, posted home from my regiment to help run what was then called the Boys' Squadron at Bovington, when I first became interested in what I call our 'ghost' roads. I mean the ancient, once busy, but now delightfully abandoned tracks that carried traffic of all sorts until the kaleidoscope of local anthill business was finally shaken, selected routes were surfaced for wheeled traffic and we settled into the road pattern in use today.

If you wonder why I call them ghost roads, the next time you find yourself taking a sudden ninety-degree turn in your car as the modern route quits a much older line, spare a glance at the departing wraith ahead of you. I can think of no better example than 'Snowdrop Corner', more properly Muston Corner, just beyond Higher Waterston and the junction with the road from Puddletown (the map reference, for precise identification, is 727959). Here, with Dorchester behind you, the Piddle Valley road takes a sharp left and the old London road, now an overgrown track, strides purposefully on ahead.

It was a rare stroke of luck for me, all those years ago, to be posted so near to home. I had no car: it was frowned on in my regiment for a subaltern to indulge in wheels before mounting himself, and my first care was to buy a horse so that I could ride between Bovington and Glanvilles Wooton whenever I had leave.

It worked famously. A saddle-bag carried essentials, and my kind parents did the occasional run by car with heavy items. Best, I fell in love with our county's ancient routes, because it was a matter of pride to ride as nearly as I could on a bee-line and, if possible, never to touch tarmac.

It was at that time that I made the acquaintance of Ronald Good's 1940 prize-winning essay, 'The Old Roads of Dorset', later developed by him into one of my most prized books. I think of that time as being one of the happiest I can remember. I loved the work but spent ages in the saddle with just the company of my horse, escaping the embarrassments and puzzles of that so over-rated thing called youth.

It didn't last. At no notice, my regiment summoned me back to serve with a squadron detached on active duty in the Middle East, they put a third pip on my shoulder and adult life began. But I never forgot those 'ghost roads', still search them out, picture their heyday traffic, treasure them, trace them, follow them when I can.

* * *

One way and another, wildlife has been forcing itself on our notice even more than it usually does, these past few months. First it was a swan, then badgers.

The swan saga started one morning when a busy farmer returning from visiting his stock, whom I met while I was bringing in our horses, mentioned that a swan seemed to be trapped behind wire in Stonylongs, the meadow where he grazed his sheep. Would I look at it, he asked, no doubt mentally scratching it off his list of 'things to do'?

It was a strange sight, this powerful and apparently uninjured bird, strutting up and down behind pig-wire that was no more than two feet high. It would seem that it had made an ill-judged landing in the closely planted young covert and was grounded, unable to hop clear, let alone to spread its wings and fly. Hissing and arching its reptilian neck, it repelled any offer of help. Delphie all but bolted when at my first visit I suggested we take a closer look.

For a couple of days we kept it supplied with food and water

and then, as we were due away one Sunday, sought help. That evening on our way home, we found no swan but a note of thanks trapped under our stable bucket. Well done, the RSPCA!

The badger story is, as I write, still ongoing. A couple of months ago a cavernous hole appeared in the road-edge of Park Lane, the improbably named route south from our village up and over the shoulder of Dungeon Hill. By any standards it was a hazard, a baby elephant trap. Reported, the hole was very promptly coned and screened, with materials that have since been drawn down into the sett by its owner.

I watch developments with interest – almost daily, as Park Lane is my 'pitch' for clearing litter – and with sympathy. I had set officialdom an appalling dilemma: two sacred cows locking horns. The imperative of maximising the badger population, at whatever cost, must surely be the only thing that trumps 'elf-'n'-safety? What can the Council possibly do? There can of course be no question of disturbing, or in any way interfering with the convenience of, a badger. When funds can be found, obviously a bypass will have to be built. I may yet live to see Park Lane become a ghost road.

OCTOBER 2010

Hedgelaying & Milking

'Locking up, locking up!' I call into what I hope is an empty church, before turning the door's massive key. I have a dread of shutting someone in there: didn't one of Edgar Allan Poe's gothic tales tell of some unfortunate getting locked in a church belfry overnight, and losing his wits? Certainly, the naughty swallows that nest precariously every returning year in a nook over the door's arch, to the discomfort of the ladies of the cleaning roster, have, some weeks back, vacated their summer quarters. Had they been still at home, they would have darted over my shoulders, squeaking indignantly at my intrusion, as I entered the porch.

I like to think that those very birds might be among the immigrants that a favourite cousin will see swooping around over the Drakensberg Mountains in Natal next month. I have just placed a ruler on my old school atlas, and make the one-way trip all of six thousand miles. What great hearts those little creatures have, what memories, and what navigation skills. Anyway, who can grudge those heroic commuters their generous lime-signature on the church porch flags? They honour us by their faithful visits (and I'm not on the cleaning roster!).

As I take the path home I am greeted by a sound that characterizes this season anywhere in the country, that of hedges being mechanically massacred. I mean no cheap criticism in that choice of word, farmers do what they have to do in an exigent world: and the work is expertly done, I often think that that massive tractor-mounted flail is handled as though it were a feather duster. However, it is impossible not to regret the passing of old-fashioned, quiet, hedge-husbandry . . . just as one rejoices

77

at noting that, here and there about the county, the practice still survives.

For my part, I know no more rewarding labour than laying a hedge, as they were all laid in this parish when we first moved here sixty years ago, but my time is my own, and I do not have to pay myself the agricultural wage. The men who did the hedging and ditching every year in those days are long gone now, but I remember some of them well. As a boy I used to watch them, hoping to pick up some of their skill, maybe helping by dragging discarded brush out of their way, as, when I'm in luck, a grandchild will do for me.

Tom Dufall did our hedges, Gerald Stainer those at Church Farm next-door. But it was Jim Ross who taught me how to clear a ditch, always to work up the ditch until that so-satisfying moment of seeing it run again, its pent-up flow finally released at the ditch's head. I still use Jim's old billhook, kindly given me by his widow: what precious things old hand-cherished agricultural implements are.

'You couldn't make a good job of a hedge unless you'd done the ditch first, and built up a good bank' my neighbour Charles Clarke tells me. Charles and his son Richard, the fifth or possibly seventh generation of the family to farm at Osehill, milk the last surviving dairy herd in the parish. There were 14 herds milked when we first settled here: one of my earliest memories of the village is of first thing each morning in school holidays being dispatched can-in-hand to collect the day's milk from the nearest dairy.

Charles told me of another old-timer, who used to do the Osehill hedges, Frank Paulley. 'He loved the work, just as I was never happier than when watching him at it. What really pleased him when he was doing a roadside hedge, was having his work admired by passers-by (I know the feeling DE). He would be out there all hours, take the brush by horse-and-cart into our woodland, where he would coppice, make faggots and thatcher's spars all summer-long'.

'Frank worked for us through all his life, from boyhood', Charles continued, consulting an old Wages Book. 'He joined us, age ten, in 1907, when he was paid one pound and ten pence a week to do the milking, which he did before and after school.'

Having spoken to his daughter, an old friend who lives just across the lane from us, and learnt from her that my father attended her father in his last illness, returning from the hunting field to sign his death certificate, I went back to the churchyard to lay a flower by his grave, and to study the inscription on its stone. It read 'In loving memory of Frank Paulley, who died 24th February 1950, aged 53 years'. If, like my father, he died sadly early, Frank Paulley's work left its mark, and is well-remembered hereabouts.

OCTOBER 2011

Winter

Snow Goose

Ludmila, a Single Mum

Ludmila, a single mum who took up a squat in our sack-store last summer, first burst on the scene one morning while my new horse, Ollie, was being shod. This big black-and-white bundle of bird suddenly erupted into the stable yard from the church path wicket and flew off noisily down the drive.

An alarmed horse can be quite alarming. With his mailed feet he makes a dangerous dancing partner; you are much safer in the saddle. New to the place and still quite unsettled (it took all of five months for him to feel at home here), Ollie seemed to say, 'So! You keep large, high-explosive birds here do you? I'm off!' I had a job re-assuring him, by which time Ludmila the Muscovy duck had disappeared.

A few days later, when I had occasion to visit my sack-store, a startled squeak – Ludmila never seemed to quack – alerted me to her presence. As I later discovered, she was brooding a clutch of eleven eggs on a nest made of my precious sacks. From that moment our life was turned upside-down, part of our every day being devoted to her needs – food, water and, as she had recently been widowed by a fox, security. We had to barricade the nest site nightly against her late husband's murderer, not to mention Toffee, the gamekeeper's cat.

As seemingly endless weeks went by, it became a question whether any of her eggs were fertile; with holiday absences looming, it was necessary to know. Her owner, from Church Farm, did a late abortion on one of the eggs, and, horror of horrors, it proved to contain an incomplete but already feathered embryo. A few days later cries of 'Let me out!' could be heard

from some of the remaining eggs, and then we had ducklings – six healthy ones and two weaklings that spent the first few nights of their life in a shoebox on the Aga.

The strangest part of this story, for me at least, was how Ludmila set up her squat without my knowing anything of it. Breeding birds are, as we all know, notoriously secretive. Every autumn the falling leaves disclose nests which have been built, and where broods have been covertly raised, almost under our noses. But it's not as if I go about the place with my eyes shut. How could Ludmila, whose camouflage is designed for the steppes, not Dorset, have escaped my notice when, like Jemima Puddleduck, 'she began to waddle about in search of a convenient dry nesting place'? She must have paid my sack-store at least eleven daily visits while making up her clutch.

Likewise, her daily routine once she was sitting involved her, at tea-time when she had turned her eggs and covered them with the down so selflessly plucked from her undercarriage, flying to the home pond for a refreshing swim. In five weeks I only actually saw her do that twice – and even then, as she made plain by her sheepish and resentful demeanour, I wasn't meant to. Only once, returning home up the drive with Ollie, did I see her squeezing through the wicket to take the surface route back to base via the church path.

One of the shoebox twins, though a bit of an ugly duckling – quite unlike its siblings in size and colour – survived and we returned it to her mother. The other was a poor thing which failed to thrive, could barely stand and I had to dispatch it: a hateful job.

At last the great day came when the mother and her brood of seven could be herded home the way she had come. Because undertakers always used to, and sometimes still do, park in our stable yard, I have always thought of the church path as 'The Way of the Dead'; many old friends have taken that route on their last journey. From now on it will be, much more cheerfully, 'Ludmila Lane'.

But here's another strange thing. When, a few weeks later, I visited the family on their pond next door, there were six almost full-grown young ducks. One, a drake, was as big as his mother, but not one of them was a bit like her: they were 'parsons' as some people round here call them (no disrespect intended, I'm sure), that is wild mallard crosses. Just one, still undersized, the surviving shoebox twin, was pure Muscovy.

DECEMBER 2008

Out Riding on Ollie

I know that not everybody is as daft about horses as I am, but if I promise not to make a habit of asking, will you come for a ride with me? I'm thinking back to the memorable Monday morning in August, when my new horse Ollie had been with us just five months and he suddenly settled, suddenly seemed to admit, 'OK, this is home, you're the boss.' Although I am not fond of psychobabble, you might say that we had at last 'bonded'.

Previously, like last year's Derby winner, who had to be chaperoned to the start by a stable-mate, when I rode Ollie out on his own he would suddenly 'plant' himself. In other words, he would take exception to something ahead, just refuse to lift a hoof and get a little bit wild and alarming should I insist on forward movement. I know this trick of old: we call it 'nappiness'. The only thing to do was to get off and lead him, but it was very wearying – he's a long way down and an even longer way up – and very trying on the patience, a commodity I am said to be rather short of.

He was always particularly suspicious of things on the road surface; he was, for instance, no fan of the graffito artists from County Hall who leave cabalistic messages for each other on the tarmac. He would have 'bad drain days', when you might suppose he expected a genie or a rattle-snake to pop out of every grating, and he would drop anchor, petrified with horror like Matron at a mattress-inspection, at any patch of damp.

Diana, as usual, said, 'Don't do anything silly!' as I left home and, although I regard doing silly things as being half the point of life, I had determined on a completely sober, risk-free ride. It was to be a circuit up to the ridgeway and back: nine miles, two hours, road and track, walking and trotting. Off we set.

As we headed south out of the village, up Park Lane and over the shoulder of Dungeon, as always with half an eye open for litter – Park Lane is my 'pitch' – it dawned on me that I was riding a different horse. Ears pricked confidently, he was walking out bold and fast. 'Alfred Brendel! Alfred Brendel!' his mailed feet on the road-metal seemed to say, I being still under the spell of that magician's farewell concert at Plush the month before.

Buckland Newton, our first Dorset home, came soon, with its useful church tower clock, past the Manor, then up Ridge Hill to join the ancient ridgeway, one of the oldest routes in Europe, onto what I call Gypsy Lane, although no map does. In my mind, as always at this spot, the receding figure of Tess is ahead of us. Is there any character in all fiction more poignant, more real, more living, than that poor accursed girl?

Do you remember how at 'four o'clock on a Sunday morning . . . (when) the snow had gone, and had been followed by a hard black frost . . . the ground ringing under her feet like an anvil', Tess took that long walk from 'Flintcomb-Ash' to 'Emminster', Plush to Beaminster. Ollie and I are at the exact place where 'she reached the edge of the vast escarpment below which stretched the loamy Vale of Blackmoor': how I treasure that sudden sight of the vale that contains my home.

Soon we are over Dogbury with its Iron Age earthworks and, if you are lucky, its ravens, and drop down to what Hardy called the Devil's Kitchen – Dogbury Gate. We have turned for home and we leave Tess behind and enter *Woodlanders* country.

We are on 'the forsaken coach-road' where Hardy first meets his reader in the first sentence of what is surely one of the loveliest of his novels. What a clever trick it was to site so much of the action of his stories on a road, his characters travelling, their lives in flux. Ollie knows, as all horses know, when he is on the way home. He strides confidently on, through the distractions of Lyon's Gate and Middlemarsh, asking no questions.

I ride on a loose rein. It is a matter of principle to me and a rule for life, an axiom of well-exercised authority. It worked very well for me in the Army and I only wish that I met it more elsewhere. Like a good soldier, Ollie returns and rewards the trust I put in him: we part at the gate of his meadow, new friends.

JANUARY 2009

Choirboys & Birdsong

Words are just another a form of music, and vice versa, or so it seems to me. I'd be pushed to say which was the more important moment in my life: when, soldiering in a lonely outpost, I first stumbled on Jane Austen, or when the great Dr Fox, after testing my voice, gave me a place in Clifton College's choir.

Douglas Fox was without doubt one of the greatest-hearted, most inspiring people I have ever met. As a young man he had been thought destined to be perhaps the best virtuoso pianist of his generation, but one day, when training for the front in the Great War, he held on to a hand-grenade too long and lost his right arm. He turned to teaching and became the Director of Music at his old school. I can never forget, never wish to forget, singing for that lion of a man for whom music was everything, nor can I ever repay what I owe him for being a signpost in my young life. What a lottery it is, the hands we fall into and the minds we come under at school!

I have a letter from him, pasted into the front of my copy of *The Oxford Companion to Music*. Writing in his spiky left-hand scrawl, he expresses the hope that I will keep up my piano and my singing. Some hope, of a horse-mad young cavalry subaltern: I never touched the piano again after leaving school. But singing was another matter. For me at least, if for no-one else, it has been a lifelong joy.

Please keep it to yourself, as I wouldn't like it to get back to my fellow-members of the PCC, but to sing my namesake's psalms, the canticles and some favourite hymns is one of the main reasons that I go to church, that and to hear and to rehearse the deathless words of Cranmer's Prayer Book and

King James's Bible, and to think of the countless times they have been told over in that dear place before. How dare some committee of cloth-eared clerics substitute their own banalities for such simple grandeur?

* * *

There's surely nothing to beat the music of the Dorset countryside when it's quiet, with no competition from traffic, aircraft or machinery; when, as it were, the conductor has rapped the music desk with his baton, and we are all ears. The sound of distant church bells, for instance, or, closer, the chink of a farrier's hammer on his anvil. But one of the best sounds at such a time, on a still evening perhaps, is that of a stockman calling to his beasts, using words, making sounds, that no doubt echoed down countless of his forebears' generations.

89

His beasts have their own music, too. For several weeks last autumn, what I presume was a lovesick heifer, 'bulling' as farmers call it, in a field near here would make the most extraordinary haunting, almost human, cries, full of complaint – outrage almost – and longing. Either she got what she wanted or she forgot about it, but one day she left off as suddenly as she had begun.

Birdsong of course delights us, until that sad day in late summer when feathers lying discarded here and there announce the moult, and all except the faithful robin and ringdove put their music by. Birdcalls are another matter. All the year round you can hardly leave this house in daylight without hearing a buzzard's plaintive mew, and the noise geese make in flight defies belief. A skein sometimes flies overhead, the individuals honking importantly to each other, from horizon to horizon, a rare delight.

I know that it is arguing against myself, but for me one of the most evocative sounds is in a sense quite alien and has no natural cause. You hear it only when the wind comes from dead west and when all else is silent. It might be when I am riding down Stock Hill Lane, the lovely old road that goes north out of this village towards Round Chimneys, my horse's clip-clop muffled by its generous verge. It is the whistle of a distant train, all of five miles away, on the single-track railway that runs so usefully from Weymouth to Bath and Bristol and stops to pick you up at the small stations on the way, but only if you signal to the driver.

To hell with flying. The sound of a distant train on a lonely, otherwise silent scene speaks to me of romance, adventure, travel, far-off places, of parting, of leaving or of coming home: most of all it reminds me of a magic time in the Appalachian Mountains in up-state New York a year or so ago . . . But that's a story for another day.

FEBRUARY 2009

The Boy & his Sword

It was early on the first morning home from holiday, back in September. I was absently dabbing cough-mixture on my Italian mosquito bites (mistaking it for TCP) and was in pensive mood. There had been a recent strong reminder of the event that shaped my life, indeed shaped the lives of all my generation and, for better or worse, made me what I am.

It was Diana who needed the cough-mixture. We were just back from a fortnight staying with family and friends in Italy and Croatia; she had come home with a cold, as one so often does from spending time with grandchildren. We were due out that day to a couple of lunch-time engagements. On waking, Diana had said that, because of her cold, she felt she ought not to wash her hair and that we couldn't go out if she didn't. The cold was evidently a severe one.

As always after a holiday, there was everything to do: grass clamouring to be cut, mutinous weeds that wouldn't normally dare to show themselves crowding my vegetable garden. But as always, the horses came first. Two of them needed to be exercised, to 'get their backs down' as we say, in other words to make sure that idleness and rich grass hadn't left them mutinous too. Riding Delphie and leading Bella, I trotted them out of the village past the Manor, over Stock Hill to Dark's Bridge, to see how that precious spot had fared during my fortnight's absence.

As I re-entered the house an hour later, I was greeted by the welcome sound of a hair-drier.

* * *

The memory that had been so prominent in my mind was of an evening spent at another, if very different favourite spot: a terrace above Santa Margherita Ligure (Italy, top left-hand side). I was looking across Tigullio's matchless bay to the lights of Rapallo, a magic scene. When I'm lucky, a train on its way to Italy's toe traverses the far shore, making a mournful cry. I once travelled that very line, all the way from Victoria Station to what Winston Churchill called the most beautiful spot on earth, Taormina in Sicily.

If I tell you that it was the evening of 3 September, you may guess of what I was thinking. In my mind's eye I saw myself, a six-year-old boy, dancing around in a Somerset garden one sunlit Sunday morning, crying defiance and death to Adolf Hitler as I stabbed the lawn with my wooden sword, a skewer illicitly stolen from the kitchen stapled to its point.

My mind also went back to the earlier war, and what the

future Grey of Fallodon, author of *The Charm of Birds*, said as he quit the Foreign Office on war's eve, when my father was seven and my mother but six years old: 'The lamps are going out all over Europe; we shall not see them lit again in our lifetime.' Thank goodness he was wrong.

In her diary on the first evening of the World War in which her family was to be such a symbol of the British spirit, the late Queen Mother wrote of her faith in the 'courage, sense of humour, and sense of right and wrong' of the British people. 'Some when, back along', as they still say round here, did not the elite, who, having taken over from the Church, prescribe the country's moral medicine, take a terrible wrong turning over the question of right and wrong?

Yet when I think of my neighbours, of country people generally, of my family, of the wider circle that I know well, and especially when I remember our servicemen and women at the seat of war, I'm full of hope: it's all there still. Happy Christmas!

DECEMBER 2009

'Lopper's Law'

I am sure that you will be familiar with 'Lopper's Law', whereby every outside job takes at least twice as long as you had hoped, and requires an implement that is still in the garden shed. Thus if you set out optimistically, secateurs in hand, you find that they are nowhere near man enough for the job and that what you need are a hedge-layer's long-handled loppers – and if you take the loppers, what is actually wanted is a saw, and so on.

A kindred law, which I have myself invented, I call 'Jolt'. It decrees that, as you settle down to a long-planned outside job, some cherished idea of improvement about the garden or further afield, your wife comes and tells you that there is 'Just one little thing' which she would like you to tackle first: a 'little thing' which, you may be quite sure, will exemplify Lopper's Law in all its severity, completely filling the time you had set aside for the job you had planned to do.

The only defence against Jolt, I find, is vagueness, not to say deviousness, when answering the question, 'What have you got planned for this afternoon?' There is no known defence against Lopper's Law.

* * *

Most horses have a mortal dread of pigs and won't go near them if they can possibly be avoided. There are various theories about why this should be so, but I myself have no doubt that the cause is religious: just about every saddle-horse that you are likely to ride in this country has Arab blood somewhere back in its pedigree. Ollie, who has now sadly returned to his owner,

is nearly clean-bred and was downright dangerous, not to say frantic, when I once rode him through the yard of the pig farm over beyond Boys Hill, in the next parish.

While Diana was away – reluctantly lent to like-minded friends to attend the European Three-Day-Event Championships at Fontainebleau – I put Delphie to the pig-test. It was a Saturday morning and I set out, as I often do, with no fixed intention as to where I would ride. I had a letter – Pony Express I call it and duly so stamped – to deliver at the Manor, but after that either Pulham was to be our destination, to save a telephone call, or Butterwick Dairy House Farm and its clamorous pigs.

When we got to the parting of the ways at Holwell Drove, I decided to let Delphie choose. On a slack rein she opted for straight ahead and the pig-test. Soon we were off the road on a bridleway, fording the Caundle Brook, and at the spot where Ollie had first sensed the pigs, heard and smelt them though still a field distant, and begun his whirling dervish act. Delphie, however, although patently slightly anxious at the whiff in the air, was a picture of lady-like deportment.

When we got to the yard, there was neither sight nor sound

of pigs, just their smell. Had they all gone to market? Frustrated in my purpose, we were headed for home when, up ahead of us on the long narrow track leading to Boys Hill, a quad-bike with a bale of straw up-front and a collie dog in attendance hove into view. There was barely room for us to pass each other, but the rider turned into a gateway, switched off his engine and waited for us.

As we drew alongside and I gave my thanks to that courteous young farmer, I saw to my amazement that he had a piglet across his lap. 'Might I,' I asked, 'introduce my horse to your passenger?' He smilingly assented. Delphie advanced, all curiosity, placidly sniffed the little creature, and we went on our way, in my case rejoicing. Not only had Delphie triumphantly passed the pig-test, but old-fashioned courtesy and the smile of the young farmer had quite banished a dark shadow that was in my mind.

Riding out of the village on a particularly treasured stretch of road that used to pass by two named and ancient oaks, Gog and Magog (there being just one left now), somebody had strewn thirty or forty pages of the *Star* newspaper on the verge and in the roadside ditch, a page to every stride. It near broke my spirit, if not my heart, to see such a thing and to wonder who could do it:

I picked them up, of course.

It had taken just one touch of old England, a young farmer's thoughtfulness and smile, to set matters right.

Newts in the Cellar,
Owls in the Fireplace

We like to think that we own this old house but, from the newts in the cellar to the sparrows in the roof, there are endless other claimants. Since we lost our beloved lurcher, Perdita, there has been an interregnum in the dog department, apart from the occasional stopover by a step-dog, a Dandie Dinmont with the unlikely name of Pippa-Nina. We go away too often to think of permanently replacing Perdie yet.

As well as newts, the cellar is home to frogs – if they aren't toads. It has also been visited at different times by a slow-worm, a mole and several hedgehogs who, however hard I try to prevent it, slither or tumble through the disused coal-chute, mostly to meet a watery end in the sump which holds the scavenger pump in the middle of the cellar floor. The old drain running to our distant boundary ditch, which must have been dug with the house's foundations, long since silted up. If ever the pump goes on strike and the water-table rises, the cellar becomes a paddling pool and I have to put on wellies to get to the ancient stone wine-bins.

The house is regularly invaded by mice of course, but what old house isn't? Diana, normally so tender-hearted with animals, keeps them in check, but now and then we hear them scuttling in the hollow walls or above the ceiling in our bedroom. There, I swear, one occasionally polishes its shoes, always of an early morning.

The most unwelcome visitors are surely bats. In a bat-free world I would from choice sleep with wide-open windows, but we daren't. Bats, with their Houdini ways of creeping in so sinisterly, Gollum-like, through the slightest crack, entirely sabotage sleep. Diana will not rest until the intruder is banished. I use a tennis racquet in this operation, which is probably a criminal offence or infringes their human rights, like saying 'Boo!' to a badger, or incommoding a burglar. Mad world!

* * *

Birds are another matter entirely. Of all unlikely things, I once held a goldcrest in my hand. If you have ever watched how those minute birds mouse round the foliage of a hedge or tree, insect-hunting, you can picture one taking a wrong turning in the wisteria and ending up in our bedroom. But it was an extraordinary, precious moment, holding that exquisite feathered thumbling for the few seconds it took to capture and release it. I can never forget the impression that the brushstroke of colour on its crown made on me.

The strangest thing about that encounter is that I have never seen goldcrests near the house. Just once, another precious memory, I saw a small squad of them working over the old yew that shelters what my mother called the Holy Trinity – the three-seater earth-closet at the far end of the garden, under the churchyard wall. I don't think that goldcrests, unlike my robin friends, are what my favourite bird book endearingly calls 'confiding'. Goldcrests, or golden-crested wrens, are not rare, but I can't have seen them more than three or four times in my life.

The strangest bird encounter that we have had in this house was with a tawny owl. Somehow it negotiated the winds in the drawing-room chimney, winds that even our sweep finds troublesome, and descended to the grate. Diana found it one day, blackened and disgruntled, caged behind the fireguard. Imagine the expensive mayhem such a large creature might have caused had it forced its own way free, fraternised with, or perhaps more likely attacked, the large pictures of birds that

hang round the walls, and indeed redecorated the whole room with soot.

I like to think that John Gould's wife, my grandmother's grandmother, with a red-footed falcon on her wrist, looked on approvingly from her portrait above the fireplace as Diana somehow, cleverly, extricated the owl and carried it to freedom. The most memorable moment of the whole extraordinary episode, as Diana tells it, is of how the bird turned its head a full 180 degrees, as owls can, and stared her accusingly and unblinkingly in the face as she marched it out of doors.

For some reason we haven't had a horse in the house yet, but an enormous lost ram, supposedly summering in our orchard, once came in at the back and left by the front door. I'll tell you about the giraffe in the drawing room another day.

FEBRUARY 2010

A Roe Deer

An early memory from when we first settled in this county after the war was of going to the South Dorset point-to-point, then held at West Morden, seeing Charborough Park's magnificent wall, and of my father saying that its building was an example of 'outdoor relief' during a time of agricultural depression. It's a strong phrase, carrying a sad picture; my young mind was struck by it, and, as you can see, it has stayed with me.

The Proms were coming to an end when I was contemplating this article, riding one Sunday morning over Dungeon Hill. Inevitably, Benson's plangent lines and Elgar's inspiring music kept coming into my head, but, as always nowadays, I had to fight against substituting my own words: 'Land of 'elf-'n'-safety…'. (If you are really kind, and read further, I shall give you the full version later.) What particularly brought such unforgivable levity to mind was recently being told of the ridiculous hoops in the shape of 'risk assessments' a friend had had to thread before being allowed to unleash his team of Lifeboat collectors on to the so dangerous streets of Dorchester.

Can you imagine a starker contrast, between heart-of-oak heroism and the piffling pettifoggery of ghastly, zombie-like bureaucracy ponderously making work out of the risky business of shaking a collecting tin – the contrast between these dear islands' best and worst, their once-upon-a-time and now?

But, in these difficult days, perhaps we shouldn't look too nearly at the employment of all of those whose salaries we pay. Ought we not instead to regard their work more charitably, as a form of 'indoor relief'?

Oh, and since you ask, the full version, which you will find fits the music very well, goes like this:

Land of Health and Safety,
Mother of PC!
Ri-i-isk assessment,
Bureaucra-a-a-cy.
Wider still and wider etc.

At about the same time, a much happier event impressed itself on my memory, bringing with it sounds and a picture that I will certainly carry to my grave.

I was up a ladder on the east wall of the house, pruning wisteria, when an eerie cry, continuously repeated and rebounding off the church tower behind me, seized my attention and had me scrambling to the ground. Diana called out that it must be a strange bird, but I knew better, having heard it once before, many years ago.

With the echo, it was quite difficult to decide the right direction to take, but soon I had it pin-pointed – through our boundary hedge, off our land into the heart of my neighbour's spinney, on ground where I had never in my life had occasion – let alone licence – to set foot before.

Sure enough, screaming for its mother, a half-grown roe deer was swimming for its life in a small, unguarded, ground-level static water tank. She was not much bigger than a spaniel. It was a matter of seconds to scoop her to safety, and lay her in a nearby patch of sunlight. I squatted, back to a tree-trunk, while she shivered, incapable of movement, her terrified eyes on me.

For fully half-an-hour she lay there, motionless apart from the shivering. I contemplated the dreadful thought of having to dispatch her – murder in cold blood, I've had to do it before, what countryman has not? Then, with a first slight movement, she tried ineffectually to re-arrange her spindly legs. Lifted to her feet, she merely let out another heart-wringing yell, and collapsed. Evidently I was part of the problem: it seemed

sensible to quit the scene.

An hour later she was gone and next day, walking one of our step-dogs, I saw her romping with her mother and brother in the adjacent meadow. Roe, as I'm sure you know, nearly always produce a 'pigeon pair'.

What stays with me – a precious memory – is the little creature lying a-shiver, soaked and helpless at my feet, as if new-born into a merciless world, an unlooked-for, strange nativity. Happy Christmas.

DECEMBER 2010

Lost & Found

This is a story of lost and found. 'Missing presumed lent . . .' read an appeal to our neighbours that I recently posted on the village notice board. The text continued '. . . one eight-foot ladder gone from our garage, and one garden sieve, ditto from the potting shed. We would be so grateful to hear news of either item.'

I was in fact putting an optimistic gloss on what seemed at the time to be rather sinister disappearances. We have had too much stolen from our outhouses too often in the past – including having the saddle-room completely emptied – to be light hearted when outdoor things suddenly go AWOL. But it was just possible – indeed all too possible these days when I have difficulty remembering what I did two minutes ago, and what that knot in my handkerchief is for – that I had lent the items to one of the said neighbours and forgotten I had done so.

As to items found, or perhaps I should call them *objets trouvés*, since it occurred to me that they might have been an 'art installation' not merely an example of fly-tipping, the work perhaps of some Eminent (forgive the pun) metropolitan artist with progressive tastes, striving to bring us yokels up-to-date. They were a lavatory pan and cistern, ornamenting the broad grass verge in otherwise-beautiful Kennels Lane, just across our parish boundary.

Thoughtless of their artistic merit, not to mention their possibly immense saleroom value – were they perhaps a Turner Prize entry? – I shifted them to Sherborne tip and unceremoniously dumped them in the rubble skip, conscious as I did so that a plumber would have to had paid to do so, and reflecting on another modern art form: that of designing laws and regulations that have almost exactly the opposite effect from what was supposedly intended?

* * *

Casting around in my timber store for a suitably stout piece for a job that needed doing in the horses' field-shelter, in a happy moment my eye was caught by a length of pew-back, rescued from the stuff chucked out after the fire in our church a couple of years ago. I knew then that I would, one day, find a use for it and that doing so would delight me: now its time had evidently come.

About six inches by two in section, chastely moulded but badly charred oak, heavy and still strong, it was a piece of the rail against which those in the pew in front would have leant when they sat back, and on which those behind them would have rested their tented hands when kneeling in prayer. A holy, storied thing – if only it could speak! – I can't tell you what pleasure it gave me to think of giving it another use and another life.

What it does now is to allow Dandy, Bella or Delphie to reach over and munch their hay, at the same time restraining them from trampling the expensive hard-won stuff. What it did then I endlessly try to imagine as I give the horses their grub. I have of course no means of knowing how long those pews stood in the de Glanville Chapel before the fire, nor where the Churchill family sat when they attended church after moving to this parish over three centuries ago, but I choose to picture the future victor of Blenheim, a small boy at prayer resting, on that very piece of blackened wood, the hands that were to shape the history of the western world.

* * *

By the way, if you are wondering about our lost property. I chanced on the missing ladder in the orchard when I went to

start picking the Bramleys. It was well above eye-level in my step-grandson Jasper's tree-house, like a knitting-needle thrust through a ball of wool . . . lucky timing, as I was able to tell the Village Meeting of my discovery that evening, before somewhat sheepishly taking down my notice.

The riddle of the sieve, as it were, was solved when I suddenly remembered when I had last used it, sifting dried soil out of the onion crop, and where I had left it. We now have two garden sieves, a sympathetic neighbour having kindly replaced the 'lost' one.

FEBRUARY 2011

One Soldier's Christmas

'Cotton wool! Cotton wool!' called out my then six-year-old son Charlie, advancing on me, pointing at my beard, as I entered the drawing-room door, sack in hand, when by some miracle the whole family was home from the Army for Christmas. I was consciously trying to re-enact a pre-war scene I remembered so well, our then gardener playing the part, but evidently my disguise was not as good as his had been.

Small children are not always so lucid with their interventions. It must have been sometime in the year following, when his mother and I went to collect Charlie's younger brother Miles after his first day at infant school, that we were met by a small knot of evidently concerned teachers. 'We are worried about Miles,' they said. 'He complains of being "complicated, very complicated".'

Offers of 'counselling' echoed in our ears as they, I fancy, rather reluctantly entrusted him to us. It didn't take long once we got him safe home to discover that it was not counselling that was needed . . . but syrup of-figs.

* * *

As I have suggested, Christmas with his family could, in the nature of Army life, not always be counted on by a soldier. One particular Christmas I remember was that of 1975, when, towards the end of my near quarter-century of regimental duty, I had the great good luck, and honour, to take my Regiment, then called the 13th/18th Royal Hussars (Queen Mary's Own), for a tour of duty in Ulster.

It was, and no doubt still is, our custom for the officers to serve the men their Christmas dinner in the cookhouse, a happy hilarious occasion, with much good-natured ribbing. My role on this occasion was, accompanied by a retinue, to seat myself at a small table, with a place set for one. The Cook Sergeant's duty was serve me the biggest plate of turkey and trimmings you ever saw; mine, somehow, to do justice to it, my small audience,

especially the Cook Sergeant, poker-faced, enjoying the joke.

Did they but know it, more fun was to come. Shortly, the Regimental Sergeant Major bent to my ear, to remind me quietly that I was expected at Armagh Gaol. Have you got there? Hardly had I entered the prison kitchen when my horrified eyes were met by an identical scene, a place-setting for one. It was clear where my duty lay, that the honour of the Regiment was at stake, but I have never sat down to Christmas dinner since without recalling the time when I had to eat two.

That Christmas, a kind friend from Charminster, having made a collection, sent us out a tea-chest of books and pastimes. I'd like to name him, it was Ian Cobbold, I wish that he were alive to read of my remembered gratitude. Amongst the treasures were several chess sets.

Did he know that our soldiers were Yorkshiremen, that many if not most of them learnt the game at school? One of the well-remembered pleasures of that tour was the game I always had on the go with our Intelligence Section. I had my father's Jaques lock-in travelling chess set, the one that travelled the oceans with him through his war.

I would make a move, place the set in my 'Out' tray, a clerk would pounce, it would re-appear accompanied by a smile in the 'In' tray. I can't remember who got the best of it, but it was such fun. A lot of soldiering involves waiting: it's as well to be ready for it: chess was a great standby.

Have I conveyed to you something of the spirit of outfit I was so lucky to be part of, that had been patient mother, brother and sister to me for all those precious years? I can never be sufficiently grateful for that Ulster tour. I felt that, as the end of my time of 'real' soldiering came into view, a stub-end of staff-service beckoning, that I was doing something really useful: helping to keep peace in that troubled province.

Of course it was nothing, absolutely nothing, to what our brave soldiers are required do across the world now. 'We' are now called The Light Dragoons, everywhere you will hear the new regiment spoken of as of amongst the finest; I am immensely proud of the connection.

So, as our peerless Armed Forces prepare to step off, 'By the left . . . Quick march', into the challenges of the coming year, let our thoughts and hearts go with them. Happy Christmas.

DECEMBER 2011